OVER 70 AMAZING RECIPES

FOR THE FESTIVE SEASON

BY AVANT-GARDE VEGAN

GAZ OAKLEY

**Photography by Simon Smith
and Peter O'Sullivan**

quadrille

VEGAN *Christmas*

INTRODUCTION

Christmas is a time for celebration and happiness. I have always loved Christmas, and growing up, my family made it very special. My dad is a great cook, and the food was always a big part of the celebrations.

When I started cooking, I took over the Christmas Day cooking responsibilities from my dad and it was a great feeling serving up my own food for the family. When I went vegan, I had to put in extra effort. I didn't want my family feeling that they were missing anything.

I have put together the ultimate vegan Christmas cookbook to help you create extravagant festive vegan food. I'm so proud of the recipes in this book and I can assure you they are all packed with incredible festive flavours. There are some real show stoppers that are guaranteed to wow all of your guests at Christmas.

At a time of happiness and peace, my goal is to get as many people's Christmas dinner tables to reflect that. The fewer animal products on dinner tables, the better, and I hope that the recipes in my book will inspire you to share my goal and achieve it yourself.

Thanks so much for purchasing my book.

MERRY CHRISTMAS!

Gaz

INGREDIENTS & EQUIPMENT

AGAR AGAR powder or flakes are a sea-vegetable gelling agent – so basically a vegan gelatine. It's brilliant stuff and can contribute to some amazing dishes!

AGAVE NECTAR is the sweet nectar extracted from several species of the agave plant, the majority of which are grown in Mexico or South Africa. It is a great natural sweetener. In my recipes, I tend to advise using either agave nectar or maple syrup, as they are very similar in terms of sweetness, however agave is often slightly more affordable.

LIQUID SMOKE This handy little flavouring is an optional ingredient in my recipes, but it's absolutely great at creating a smoky flavour.

MISO PASTE Made from fermented soy beans, this paste has a superstrong umami flavour. You can find it in the Asian section of most supermarkets. It's a staple ingredient in Japanese cooking. Soy-free miso pastes can be found – made from rice. Alternatively, you can replace it with things like tomato purée (paste), coconut aminos or Marmite. If a recipe calls for white miso, just leave the miso out completely.

NORI is made by shredding edible seaweed and then pressing it into thin sheets. It's often used when making sushi.

NUTRITIONAL YEAST is a deactivated yeast. It has a strong flavour that is quite nutty, cheesy and creamy, which makes it the perfect ingredient in my vegan "cheese" recipes and lots of other recipes where I need a bold flavour.

SEITAN, or vital wheat gluten. This is a food made from gluten – the main protein of wheat. This product has been used in vegetarian recipes for years (Buddhist monks used it as a meat replacement) and it's often used in Asian cookery. I have modernized many ancient recipes to produce some stunning dishes. I love creating dishes with wheat gluten!

TAPIOCA STARCH Tapioca is extracted from the cassava root. This magic starch gives my "cheeses" a great stringy, cheese-like texture.

TOFU is the first vegan protein people think of. I have some incredible ways to turn this often-boring product into something spectacular. Also known as beancurd, it is cultivated by coagulating soy milk and then pressing the resulting curds into soft, white blocks. Tofu can be soft, firm, or extra firm. I use firm tofu in all the recipes in my book.

POWERFUL BLENDER One of the most important pieces of equipment in a good vegan kitchen is a powerful blender and lots of my recipes rely on one. I promise that it will be a rally good investment! I recommend a Ninja Kitchen System.

Christmas

MORNING

Streaky "BACON"

The most incredible vegan "bacon" you will taste. It's definitely worth all the effort, and is a key element in my No-turkey (page 64) and No pigs in blankets (page 92) recipes.

FOR THE "BACON"

WET INGREDIENTS
240ml (1 cup) vegetable stock
120ml (½ cup) apple juice
10g (½ cup) dried mushrooms
2 tbsp soy sauce
5 tbsp maple syrup
1 tbsp miso paste
4 tbsp sweet smoked paprika
2 tbsp liquid smoke
1 red onion, finely chopped
 and sautéed
2 garlic cloves, finely chopped
 and sautéed
100g (½ cup) tinned chickpeas
 (garbanzos), drained
1 tsp dried sage
½ tsp fennel seeds
1 tsp sea salt
1 tsp black pepper

DRY INGREDIENTS
300g (2¼ cups) vital wheat gluten
4 tbsp chickpea (gram) flour
3 tbsp nutritional yeast

FOR THE "STREAK"

WET INGREDIENTS
80g (½ cup) firm tofu
120ml (½ cup) soy milk
 (or other non-dairy milk)
100g (½ cup) canned chickpeas
 (garbanzos), drained
1 tsp onion salt
¼ tsp garlic powder
1 tsp dried tarragon
1 tbsp white miso paste
1 tsp white pepper

DRY INGREDIENTS
130g (1 cup) vital wheat gluten
2 tbsp chickpea (gram) flour
1 tbsp nutritional yeast

Makes
**Around
20 rashers**

Cooks In
180 minutes

Difficulty
7/10

STREAKY "BACON" RECIPE CONTINUED

Place all the wet ingredients for the "bacon" into a food processor and blitz together.

Combine all the dry ingredients for the "bacon" in a large mixing bowl, add the blitzed wet ingredients and mix together to form a dough, then tip the dough out on to a clean work surface.

Knead well for 12 minutes, either by hand or in an electric stand mixer with a dough hook attachment. It's really important that you knead the dough properly – if you don't your finished "bacon" will be soft and spongy. After 12 minutes of kneading, set the dough aside to rest at room temperature.

Blitz together all the wet ingredients for the "streak".

Combine all the dry ingredients for the "streak" in a large clean mixing bowl, add the blitzed wet ingredients and mix together to form a dough, then tip it out on to a clean work surface.

Knead by hand, or use a stand mixer, for 4–6 minutes.

Roll and bash the "bacon" dough using a rolling pin until it's approximately A4-paper-sized. Do the same with the "streak" dough, then lay the streak dough on top of the "bacon" dough and cut the doughs in half. Place one half on top of the other and roll/bash the doughs together until you have a rectangle about 4cm (1½in) thick.

Generously sprinkle sea salt over the dough rectangle and set aside. Set a large saucepan of water over a medium heat to simmer.

Wrap the dough tightly in greaseproof paper and then in cling film (plastic wrap). Make sure it is well sealed, then lower the wrapped dough into the water to simmer for 2 hours, flipping over half way through cooking.

After 2 hours remove the "bacon" from the water and leave until cool enough to handle. Unwrap the "bacon", transfer to a plate and put it in the fridge to cool completely (about 4 hours).

Once chilled, slice the "bacon" to the thickness of your choice. You can eat it cold or pan fry, grill or bake it until golden and crisp. It keeps in the fridge for around a week and can also be frozen for up to 3 months.

Caramelized
BANANAS

Banana and peanut butter are a match made in heaven. Even better when you caramelize the banana! This is a perfect start to Christmas Day – and also very quick and simple to make!

1 tbsp coconut oil
3 bananas, cut into slices,
 at an angle
2 tbsp coconut sugar
2 tbsp peanut butter
2 slices toast (or gluten-free bread
 or rice cakes)

TO SERVE
fresh mint leaves
zest of 1 lime
handful of walnuts
handful of blueberries
handful of coconut flakes
1 tbsp maple syrup

Serves
2

Cooks In
25 minutes

Difficulty
2/10

GFO
**If gluten-free
bread is used**

Place a heavy based non-stick frying pan over a medium heat. Add the coconut oil, wait for it to melt, then add the banana slices. Fry for 3 minutes on each side, until they're nicely caramelized. Sprinkle over the coconut sugar whilst they are cooking.

Spread the peanut butter generously onto the two slices of toast and top with the caramelized banana.

Divide the toppings between the two, finishing with a drizzle of maple syrup.

TOFU BENEDICT

Wow your guests with this beautiful breakfast, it's a real show stopper.
The "hollandaise" is velvety and smooth, the perfect match for smoky tofu.

225g (8oz) block firm smoked
  tofu, pressed to remove water
2 tbsp rapeseed oil, for frying
pinch of black salt (optional for an
  "eggy" flavour, or use sea salt)
pinch of ground pepper

FOR THE "HOLLANDAISE" SAUCE
120ml (½ cup) soy milk
3 tbsp white wine vinegar
½ tsp English mustard
pinch of sea salt and pepper
120ml (½ cup) rapeseed oil

FOR THE SAUTÉED SPINACH
4 big handfuls of baby spinach
pinch of sea salt and pepper

TO SERVE
2 breakfast muffins or bagels
small bunch of fresh chives,
  finely chopped
pinch of cress
handful of cherry tomatoes, halved

Serves
2

Cooks In
35 minutes

Difficulty
5/10

GFO
**If gluten-free
bread is used**

First up, make the "hollandaise" sauce. Pour the soy milk, vinegar, mustard and seasoning
into a measuring jug and blend using an electric stick blender, until mixed well. Keep
the blender running and slowly trickle in the oil until the sauce starts to thicken up. Once
you've added all the oil it should be thick and creamy but still pourable. If your sauce is
too thick stir in a few additional tablespoons of soy milk. Taste to check the seasoning.
Cover the sauce with cling film (plastic wrap) and refrigerate until you're ready to serve.

Cut the tofu into rounds using an 8cm (3in) cutter. Pat dry with kitchen paper then preheat
a non-stick frying pan over a medium heat. Add the oil to the pan. Pan fry the tofu until
golden on each side, around 3–4 minutes. Season with the black salt, if using, and pepper.

Remove the tofu from the pan and set aside. Turn the heat up high and add a touch
more oil. When it starts to smoke add all the spinach (don't worry, it will wilt down
quickly). Cook the spinach for 1 minute, stirring quickly. Season with a pinch of salt and
pepper, then remove from the heat. Spinach contains lots of water, so I always press it
with a clean kitchen towel to soak up any excess liquid.

Toast the muffins or bagels, if you like, then add the tofu slices and sautéed spinach.
Scatter around the cherry tomato halves. Top with a dollop of the "hollandaise" sauce,
sprinkle over some chopped chives, top with a pinch of cress and serve immediately.

Sweet Potato
WAFFLES
WITH SAUTÉED MUSHROOMS

Cook the potato the day before to speed up the process on Christmas Day.
Light and savoury - these make a great sharing breakfast.

FOR THE WAFFLES
2 tbsp chia seeds, blitzed to a
 fine powder
160g (5½oz) cooked sweet potato
120g (1 cup) buckwheat flour
45g (½ cup) chickpea (gram) flour
360ml (1½ cups) non-dairy milk
2 tsp baking powder
1 tsp onion salt
2 tbsp maple syrup
¼ tsp cayenne pepper
handful of fresh chives
oil, for greasing

FOR THE MUSHROOMS
2 tbsp rapeseed oil
300g (10½oz) mushrooms
 of your choice
handful of cherry tomatoes
handful of chopped fresh parsley
pinch of sea salt and pepper

TO SERVE
1 avocado, peeled and sliced
3 tbsp mixed seeds

Serves
2

Cooks In
45 minutes

Difficulty
5/10

GF

Measure the waffle ingredients into a blender and blend on a medium speed until fully combined. You may need to stop, scrape the sides and stir the mixture a couple of times. It should be the consistency of a thick batter. If it is too thick, add a little more milk.

Preheat a waffle pan or machine to a medium temperature and lightly grease with oil. If your machine or pan is too hot the middle of the waffle won't cook. When your waffle pan has reached temperature, pour in the batter (use a ladle) and leave the waffle pan to work its magic for 10–12 minutes. Cooking times may vary depending on your type of waffle pan or machine. Once your waffles are golden brown and quite firm to the touch, they are cooked – remove and keep warm in a preheated oven (150°C/300°F). Lightly grease the pan/machine before repeating with the remainder of the batter.

While the waffles are cooking, heat a non-stick frying pan over a low heat and add the rapeseed oil. Sauté the mushrooms for 4–5 minutes, tossing the pan regularly. Once they are golden, throw in the tomatoes, parsley and seasoning and cook for 2–3 minutes. Once the mushrooms and all the waffles are cooked, serve immediately with some sliced avocado on the side. Sprinkle over the mixed seeds.

PARTY

food & light

meals

Smoked "Salmon"
WITH "CREAM CHEESE", CAPERS AND DILL CANAPÉS

Back at it again with the nori! This time for the perfect canapé. Marinating for 24 hours allows the smoky flavours to be fully absorbed by the carrot.

FOR THE SMOKED "SALMON"
440ml (scant 2 cups) vegetable stock
1 tbsp miso paste
3 tbsp sweet smoked paprika
1 large sheet of nori
2 tbsp maple syrup
2 tbsp smoked sea salt (or regular sea salt)
juice of 1 lemon
5 large carrots, peeled

FOR THE "CREAM CHEESE"
125g (½ cup) raw cashew nuts
2 tbsp lemon juice

pinch of sea salt and white pepper
1 tbsp nutritional yeast
110ml (½ cup) filtered water

TO SERVE
6 slices of toasted rye bread (or a gluten-free bread), cut into small pieces for canapés
lemon slices
3 tbsp capers
small handful of fresh dill

Serves
6

Cooks In
20 minutes

Difficulty
2/10

GFO
If gluten-free bread is used

Place all the smoked "salmon" ingredients except the carrots into a medium saucepan, bring to the boil, then lower to a simmer for 10 minutes to let the flavours infuse.

While the broth is cooking, use a peeler to slice the carrots into long ribbons and place them in a large heatproof bowl.

Pour the broth through a sieve directly over the carrots into the bowl. This will lightly cook them. When the broth has cooled, cover the bowl with cling film (plastic wrap) or place the mixture into sterilized jars. Refrigerate for at least a day (or up to seven days). The broth acts as a marinade.

To make the "cream cheese", soak the nuts in boiling water for 15 minutes. Drain away the soaking water and tip the nuts into a blender cup with the rest of the ingredients. Simply blitz everything until smooth, then use straight away or store in the fridge for 3–4 days.

To serve, generously spread the "cream cheese" onto pieces of toasted bread, top with the smoked "salmon" (drained of marinade), then top with lemon, capers and dill.

"SCALLOPS"

WITH CRISPY "BACON", PEA PURÉE AND

Taste-of-the-sea Foam

With the taste-of-the-sea flavour and succulent texture of the mushroom "scallops" this will impress anyone you cook it for... not to forget the awesome crunchy rice-paper "bacon".

FOR THE "SCALLOPS"
5 king oyster (trumpet) mushrooms
rapeseed oil, for frying

FOR THE BROTH
rapeseed oil, for sautéing
1 shallot, finely sliced
1 garlic clove, finely sliced
200ml (7fl oz) white wine
400ml (1¾ cups) vegetable stock
1 sheet of nori, cut into 4 pieces
sprig of fresh thyme
juice of 1 lemon

FOR THE "BACON"
5 sheets edible rice paper
3 tbsp maple syrup
2 tbsp soy sauce or coconut aminos
2 tbsp miso paste
1 tbsp coconut oil
2 tsp smoked paprika

FOR THE PEA PURÉE
1 shallot
260g (2 cups) frozen peas
125ml (½ cup) white wine
60ml (¼ cup) vegetable stock
pinch of sea salt and pepper

FOR THE TASTE-OF-THE-SEA FOAM
125ml (½ cup) "scallop" broth
250ml (1 cup) soy or oat cream
½ tsp liquid smoke (optional)
2 tbsp lemon juice
1 tsp xanthan gum

TO SERVE
cress
lemon zest
handful of cooked peas

Serves
4

Cooks In
75 minutes

Difficulty
5/10

GF

Preheat your oven to 180°C (350°F). Line two baking sheets with non-stick baking paper.

First up, the "scallops". Remove the tops from the king oyster mushrooms (save these for a stir fry, perhaps), wash the stems, then slice into 2.5cm (1in) discs.

Add a little oil to a medium saucepan and set over a medium heat, then sauté the shallot with the garlic until soft.

"SCALLOPS" RECIPE CONTINUED

Add the white wine and let it bubble for a minute or so to cook off the alcohol, then add the stock and the rest of the broth ingredients. Simmer for 2–3 minutes, then add the mushroom discs and poach them for 10 minutes. Once cooked, remove the mushrooms from the broth with a slotted spoon and place on a plate lined with kitchen paper to dry off. Continue to simmer the broth so it reduces down.

Next, the "bacon" – using scissors cut the rice paper into rasher-sized strips and set aside. Mix together the rest of the "bacon" ingredients in a small bowl and half fill another bowl with boiling water.

Pick up two strips of rice paper and dip them into the hot water for 30 seconds or until lightly softened, shake off any excess water, then dip the strips into the marinade mixture, making sure they are well covered. Lay the strips onto one of the lined baking sheets and repeat with the rest of the rice paper strips.

Bake the coated strips for 8–10 minutes. Keep a close eye, though, as they can burn quickly. Remove the tray from the oven and set aside – the "bacon" will crisp up as it cools. Leave the oven on.

Next make the pea purée. Sweat the shallots until soft in a small saucepan, add the frozen peas and allow them to defrost, stirring. Add the wine, stock and seasoning and cook the peas for 3 minutes. Remove from the heat, let it cool a little, then use a hand stick blender to blitz to a smooth purée. Set aside until you're ready to serve.

Preheat a non-stick frying pan over a medium heat ready to sear your "scallops". While the pan is heating, prepare the foam – strain 125ml (½ cup) of the reduced mushroom broth into a medium saucepan, add the soy or oat cream, liquid smoke and lemon juice and stir over a low heat to combine.

Add a glug of rapeseed oil and sear your "scallops" in the frying pan for 2–3 minutes each side, until golden, transferring them to a lined baking sheet as you go, then pop them into your oven for 5 minutes.

Remove the scallops from the oven and take the broth/cream off the heat. Add the xanthan gum to the foam and blitz it for a minute with a hand blender to create some foam.

Plate up the "scallops", with plenty of pea purée, crispy "bacon" and foam. Garnish with a little cress and lemon zest and sprinkle over a few of the cooked peas.

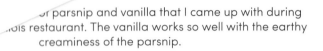

...r parsnip and vanilla that I came up with during ...ois restaurant. The vanilla works so well with the earthy creaminess of the parsnip.

2 tbsp rapeseed oil or water
4 banana shallots, finely chopped
1 garlic clove
8 parsnips, peeled and chopped into
 2cm (¾in) pieces
2 sprigs of fresh thyme
440ml (scant 2 cups) vegetable stock
440ml (scant 2 cups) almond milk
1 vanilla pod

3 tbsp lemon juice
sea salt and pepper

TO SERVE
60g (½ cup) hazelnuts
50g (½ cup) dried cranberries
a few sprigs of fresh thyme
 or rosemary
good olive oil

Serves
6

Cooks In
40 minutes

Difficulty
2/10

GF

Heat the oil or water in a saucepan over a medium heat, then sweat the shallots and garlic until translucent. Add some seasoning, the parsnips and thyme sprigs.

Turn the heat down very low and cover the saucepan. Sweat the parsnips until they're almost soft, stirring often – for about 15 minutes.

Add the stock and milk, and stir to combine. Spilt the vanilla pod down the middle lengthways and scrape out the seeds using the back of your knife. Add the seeds and the pod to the saucepan, bring the soup to the boil, then take it off the heat and scoop out the vanilla pod.

Carefully pour the soup into a blender and blend until smooth. Pour the soup back into your saucepan and check the seasoning, adding salt, pepper and the lemon juice to bring out the flavours.

Serve in warmed bowls or mugs, sprinkled with the hazelnuts and cranberries, a sprig or two of herbs and drizzle of good-quality olive oil.

Butternut-squash
ARANCINI
FILLED WITH "MOZZARELLA"

One of my favourite party dishes. These crispy risotto balls fire!
Use gluten-free breadcrumbs if you prefer.

FOR THE RISOTTO
½ large butternut squash
2 tbsp olive oil
3 banana shallots, finely chopped
2 garlic cloves, crushed
200g (2 cups) risotto rice
240ml (1 cup) vegan-friendly
 white wine
1l (4¼ cups) hot vegetable stock,
 plus a little extra
2 tbsp nutritional yeast (optional)
10 sun-blushed tomatoes, chopped
handful of chopped parsley
1 tbsp chopped preserved lemon
 (optional)
50g (½ cup) panko or gluten-free
 breadcrumbs
sea salt and pepper

FOR COATING
100g (1 cup) chickpea (gram) flour
120g (2 cups) panko breadcrumbs

FOR THE "MOZZARELLA"
120g (½ cup) raw cashew nuts
120ml (½ cup) filtered cold water
120ml (½ cup) cold non-dairy milk
4 tbsp tapioca starch
2 tbsp nutritional yeast
¼ tsp dried onion powder
1 tsp white miso
1 tsp lemon juice
pinch of sea salt and white pepper
¼ tsp garlic powder
2l (8½ cups) vegetable oil, if frying

FOR THE CRISPY SAGE
10 fresh sage leaves
3 tbsp rapeseed oil

TO SERVE
Cranberry and orange sauce
 (see page 112)

Makes
**8–10 large
arancini**

Cooks In
120 minutes

Difficulty
5/10

GFO
**If gluten-free
breadcrumbs
are used**

Roast the squash before making the risotto or start the risotto half an hour into the roasting time. To cook the squash, preheat the oven to 180°C (350°F), slice the butternut squash in half lengthways and scoop out the seeds. Rub the cut surface with vegetable oil and place cut-side down on a baking sheet. Roast for 1 hour until soft. When the squash is roasted, remove from the oven and leave to cool. Scoop out the flesh into a bowl.

To make the risotto, heat the olive oil in a large saucepan over a medium heat and sauté the onion and garlic, until softened. Stir often and make sure they don't burn.

BUTTERNUT-SQUASH ARANCINI RECIPE CONTINUED

Once the onions are soft, lower the heat and add all the risotto rice. Stir well for around 1 minute, making sure the rice is thoroughly coated.

Pour in the white wine and stir every now and then until it has all been absorbed into the rice. Once it's been soaked up, add a ladleful of stock, stir well and when this has been absorbed add another ladleful, repeating until you have used up all the stock – this will take about 20 minutes. The rice should now look almost creamy. Check the rice is cooked – if it isn't, add a splash more stock, and carry on cooking for a bit.

Once the rice is soft enough to eat, gently stir in the cooked squash and the nutritional yeast. Check the risotto seasoning and add salt and pepper to taste.

Line a large baking tray with greaseproof paper and spread the risotto out over the tray. Leave it to cool for 30 minutes before chilling in the fridge for at least 2 hours.

While the risotto is cooling, make your "mozzarella". To quick soak the nuts: simply pop them in a heatproof container and pour over boiling water. Leave for around 20 minutes to soak while you measure out the other ingredients.

Once the nuts have softened, drain and add them to a high-speed blender with all the other "mozzarella" ingredients. Blend on full speed until you have a smooth mixture. I know it doesn't look anything like mozzarella now but bear with it!

Scrape the mixture into a non-stick saucepan, arm yourself with a spatula and start stirring over a medium heat. Be patient – you will be stirring for around 8–10 minutes. Stir until it is super-thick and starts to come away from the sides of the saucepan, then remove from the heat and scrape the mixture into a sandwich bag. Set aside until you're ready to fill your arancini.

Once the rice is thoroughly chilled, scrape it into a mixing bowl and add the chopped tomatoes, parsley, preserved lemon (if using) and the breadcrumbs. Mix carefully until incorporated, then divide the risotto mixture into approximately 100g (3½oz) balls. I like to make evenly sized balls, so grab your scales.

Cut a corner off a plastic sandwich bag to create a mini-piping bag, so you can squeeze out the "mozzarella".

Lightly wet your hands (to stop the rice from sticking), then poke your thumb into the middle of each rice ball and squeeze in around two teaspoons of "mozzarella". Mould the rice mixture around the mozzarella to seal it in, then repeat until you've filled all the balls.

Now you're ready to coat the arancini. In a small bowl, mix the chickpea flour with enough water to give it a sticky egg-like consistency. Put the breadcrumbs into another bowl. Carefully dip each arancini into the wet flour mixture, then gently roll in the breadcrumbs, making sure each one is well coated, then transfer to a plate as you go. Repeat until you've coated all the balls.

Either heat the oven to 180°C (350°F) then bake the arancini on a lined baking tray for 15 minutes or you can fry them. I set my deep-fat fryer to 170°C (340°F) and fry them for 4 minutes, or until golden and crisp.

Quickly fry the sage leaves in the oil that you're frying your arancini in or, if baking, simply heat a non-stick frying pan over a medium heat, add a touch of oil, then fry the sage leaves for a few seconds until crisp. Transfer to a plate lined with kitchen paper to drain.

Serve the hot arancini straight away with the crispy sage and my cranberry sauce alongside!

Sweet
CRANBERRY
GLAZED BBQ
"RIBS"

I unleashed this recipe on my YouTube channel to rave reviews! This slightly refined version makes perfect party food or starter.

FOR THE "RIBS"
WET INGREDIENTS
300ml (1¼ cups) hot vegetable stock
10g (½ cup) dried mushrooms
1 tbsp vegetable oil
1 onion, finely chopped
2 garlic cloves, finely chopped
100g (½ cup) chickpeas (garbanzos)
3 tbsp tomato purée
1 tbsp soy sauce
1 tbsp maple syrup
1 tbsp miso
2 tsp liquid smoke
¼ tsp sea salt
¼ tsp pepper
3 tsp smoked paprika
1 tsp fennel seeds
½ tsp allspice
1 tbsp chilli flakes

DRY INGREDIENTS
290g (2¼ cups) vital wheat gluten
30g (¼ cup) chickpea (gram) flour
2 tbsp vegetable oil, for griddling

FOR THE CRANBERRY BBQ SAUCE
225g (1 cup) tomato ketchup
2 tsp English mustard
1 tbsp balsamic vinegar
4 tbsp Cranberry and orange sauce
 (page 112)
2 drops liquid smoke (optional)
3 tbsp coconut sugar
1 tbsp cumin
1 tsp garlic powder
½ tsp allspice
sea salt and pepper
360ml (1½ cups) cola
1 bay leaf
1 star anise

Serves
8

Cooks In
180 minutes

Difficulty
7/10

"RIBS" RECIPE CONTINUED

Preheat your oven to 160°C (325°F).

Mix the hot vegetable stock with the dried mushrooms in a small bowl and set aside for 5 minutes for the mushrooms to rehydrate.

Heat the oil in a small saucepan, sauté the onion and garlic until softened and lightly golden, then spoon into a blender with all the other wet ingredients, plus the mushrooms and stock. Blitz until smooth.

Mix the vital wheat gluten and chickpea flour together in a large mixing bowl. Pour in the wet mixture and stir with a spatula until everything is well combined and forms a dough.

Tip the dough onto a clean work surface and knead for around 12 minutes. Be firm – the tougher you are, the more meat-like texture your "ribs" will have when cooked. Once kneaded, leave the dough to rest for around 10 minutes.

Mix together the BBQ sauce ingredients, except the cola, bay leaf and star anise, in a large bowl.

Shape the "rib" dough into a rectangle around 1cm (½in) thick and cut down the middle.

Preheat a griddle pan over a high heat and add the two tablespoons of oil. Brush some BBQ sauce over each piece of dough and lay these on the pan to grill for 2–3 minutes on each side. Try to get some nice char lines. You may need to grill one piece of dough at a time but once both pieces are charred, transfer them to a deep baking dish.

Mix the cola into the remaining BBQ sauce, then pour it over the dough. Add the bay leaf and star anise. Bake in the oven for 2 hours, carefully turning over the pieces of dough half way through cooking. Add a little water to the tray to stop the sauce from thickening too much. Once the "ribs" are cooked, remove the tray from the oven and leave to cool. I prefer to chill mine in the fridge overnight, then heat up in the oven for 10 minutes before serving as the "ribs" will be firmer and more meat-like but you can also enjoy them straight from the oven.

Slice the "ribs" before serving and spoon the sauce over the top.

Welsh RAREBITS

I was really pleased when I veganized this classic. I'm proud to be Welsh...
if you hadn't guessed! This is our fancy "cheese" on toast – super addictive.

FOR THE "CHEESE"
120g (¾ cup) raw cashew nuts
120ml (½ cup) filtered cold water
120ml (½ cup) cold non-dairy milk
3 tbsp tapioca starch
3 tbsp nutritional yeast
1 tsp English mustard
1 tsp white miso
3 tbsp beer (preferably Welsh!)
pinch of sea salt and white pepper
¼ tsp onion powder

FOR THE CARAMELIZED RED ONIONS
2 tbsp rapeseed oil or water
3 red onions, peeled, halved and
 finely sliced
4 tbsp coconut or brown sugar
3 tbsp balsamic vinegar
2 sprigs of fresh thyme,
 leaves chopped
pinch of sea salt and pepper

1 baguette, cut into thick slices
 on an angle, toasted

Serves
4

Cooks In
45 minutes

Difficulty
5/10

GFO
**If gluten-free
bread is used**

First, quick soak the cashews – pop them in a heatproof bowl and pour over just
enough boiling water to cover them. Set aside for around 15 minutes to soften.

Meanwhile, make the caramelized onions. Heat the oil or water in a heavy-based
saucepan over a medium heat, then add the onions. Cook for 3–4 minutes, stirring
often, until they start to soften and colour.

Add the sugar, vinegar, thyme and seasoning, stir well and turn the heat down very low.
Cover the saucepan and allow the onions to caramelize for 15 minutes – stir/shake the
pan every now and then.

Drain the nuts and add them to a blender with all the other "cheese" ingredients. Blend on
full speed until you have a smooth mixture.

Pour the mixture into a non-stick saucepan over a medium heat and stir with a spatula.
Be patient – you will be stirring for around 8 minutes. Keep stirring until the mixture is thick
but still pourable. Turn on your grill and line a baking sheet with baking paper. Arrange
the toasted slices of bread on the tray and generously pour over the "cheese" mix.
Place under the grill for 3–4 minutes, or until nicely caramelized.

Serve straight away with plenty of caramelized red onions.

Mini
SAUSAGE ROLLS

I couldn't not put sausage rolls in my party section!
These are best served with my Horseradish sauce (page 112).

FOR THE SAUSAGE
WET INGREDIENTS
180ml (¾ cup) hot vegetable stock
3 tbsp dried mixed mushrooms
1 tbsp vegetable oil
1 medium red onion, peeled
  and chopped
2 garlic cloves, crushed
120ml (½ cup) cider or apple juice
50g (½ cup) tinned chickpeas
  (garbanzos), drained
  and rinsed
1 tbsp tomato purée (paste)
2 tbsp paprika
1 tbsp dried sage
1 tbsp dried rosemary
zest of 1 lemon
1 tbsp dried oregano
1 tbsp dried thyme
1 tbsp dried tarragon
1 tbsp cayenne pepper
¼ tsp fennel seeds

1 tsp sea salt and pepper
2 tbsp white miso paste

DRY INGREDIENTS
260g (2 cups) vital wheat gluten
3 tbsp chickpea (gram) flour,
  plus extra for dusting
320g (11¼oz) block ready-made
  vegan puff pastry

FOR THE GLAZE
3 tbsp maple syrup
2 tbsp vegetable oil
2 tbsp non-dairy milk

FOR THE TOPPINGS
1 tbsp smoked sea salt flakes
1 tbsp fennel seeds
3 tbsp mixed sesame seeds

TO SERVE
Horseradish sauce (page 112)

Makes
8

Cooks In
120 minutes

Difficulty
7/10

Pour the hot vegetable stock into a blender, add the dried mushrooms and leave for
5 minutes for the mushrooms to rehydrate.

Meanwhile, heat the tablespoon of oil in a small saucepan and sauté the onion and
garlic until softened and lightly golden, then add to the mushrooms and stock in the
blender. Add the remaining wet ingredients and blitz until smooth.

Combine the wheat gluten and chickpea flour in a large mixing bowl. Pour in the wet
mixture and quickly stir with a spatula until everything is well combined to form a dough.
Tip the dough onto a clean work surface and knead for around 10 minutes (or use an

MINI SAUSAGE ROLLS RECIPE CONTINUED

electric stand mixer fitted with a dough hook). The tougher you are when kneading, the more of a bite your sausages will have when cooked, so be firm! Once kneaded, divide the dough into 8. I weigh each piece to make sure my sausages are all a similar size – aim for around 110g (4oz) per sausage. If you are making the sausages for the No pigs in blankets on page 94, make 16 half-size sausages.

Half fill a large, lidded saucepan with water and heat until boiling, then reduce the heat so that the water is simmering.

Prepare 8 pieces of foil, shiny-side up, approximately 25cm (10in) long. (Alternatively use greaseproof baking paper.) Roll a piece of dough into a sausage shape with your hands, then roll up in a piece of foil, twisting each end to seal. Repeat until you've wrapped all the sausages, then wrap each in cling film (plastic wrap).

Lower the wrapped sausages into the simmering water, pop the lid on and simmer for 50 minutes. Don't let the water boil – keep at a constant slow simmer – and give them a stir every now and then.

After 50 minutes, the sausages should be firm to the touch – carefully lift one out to check (they will be very hot!). If it is still soft, wrap it up and pop it back in the water to cook for a further 10 minutes. Once cooked, lift the sausages out of the pan and onto a wire rack. When they are cool enough to handle, remove the wrappings and leave to cool completely, then refrigerate until using or freeze. They will keep for 3 months in the freezer. Defrost fully before use.

Preheat the oven to 180°C (350°F) and line a baking sheet with baking parchment. Roll out the puff pastry on a floured surface until you have a long rectangle about 3mm (⅛in) thick. Cut around the edges so they are straight. Arrange the sausages in a long line in the middle of the pastry.

Mix the ingredients for the glaze together in a small bowl, then use a pastry brush to brush the pastry all around the sausages. Fold over the pastry carefully, pressing it onto the sausage so there's no trapped air, and pinch the edges together to make sure they're sealed properly. You should now have a gigantic sausage roll. Brush more glaze over the top and sprinkle on the salt, fennel seeds and sesame seeds.

Cut into 5-cm (2-in) sausage rolls and place on the lined baking sheet, then bake for 15–18 minutes, or until the pastry is golden. Serve warm with my Horseradish sauce on the side.

"Fish" Finger
SLIDERS
WITH SRIRACHA MAYO

I love these mini burgers, perfect for kids too! If you don't have time to make your own sliders, use shop-bought rolls.

FOR THE SLIDER BUNS
120ml (½ cup) almond milk
120ml (½ cup) water
1 tsp dried yeast
4 tbsp olive oil
260g (2 cups) strong white bread
 flour, plus extra for dusting
pinch of sea salt

FOR THE GLAZE
2 tbsp almond milk
2 tbsp extra virgin olive oil
1 tbsp agave nectar
4 tbsp mixed sesame seeds
pinch of sea salt

FOR THE "FISH" FINGERS
320g (11¼oz) block firm tofu,
 drained, patted dry and cut
 into fingers
2 nori sheets, cut to similar size
 as the tofu

juice of 1 lemon
2 tsp sea salt
90g (¾ cup) chickpea (gram) flour
120ml (½ cup) water
50g (1 cup) chickpea (garbanzo)
 crumbs or panko

FOR GAZ'S SRIRACHA MAYO
120ml (½ cup) unsweetened soy milk
1 tsp white wine vinegar
1 tsp lemon juice
240ml (1 cup) rapeseed oil
pinch of sea salt and white pepper
1 tbsp Sriracha (or more, to taste)

TO SERVE
½ cucumber, sliced into ribbons
10 radishes, finely sliced
12 cocktail gherkins
small handful of fresh parsley

Makes
12 sliders

Cooks In
60 minutes

Difficulty
5/10

GFO
If chickpea crumbs and gluten-free bread are used

First up, the buns. Line two baking sheets with non-stick baking parchment. Heat the milk and water together in a small saucepan until lukewarm, then remove from the heat and whisk in the yeast. Leave for 10 minutes until it's slightly bubbly, then add the olive oil.

Meanwhile, place the flour and salt in a large mixing bowl and make a well in the middle. Pour the milk mixture into the well, stirring with a wooden spoon as you pour. Stir until the dough starts combining, then bring together with your hands to form a dough.

Tip the dough onto a lightly floured work surface and knead for around 10 minutes.

"FISH" FINGER SLIDERS RECIPE CONTINUED

The dough should be smooth and quite elastic. Lightly oil the mixing bowl (so the dough won't stick) and place the dough back in. Lay a clean damp tea-towel over the top of the bowl and leave somewhere warm for around 1 hour, or until the dough has doubled in size.

After an hour, remove the dough from the bowl. It should feel beautiful and light. (I love this part.) Knock the dough back and knead it lightly for around 4 more minutes.

Divide the dough into 12 equal pieces and roll each piece into a ball. Use scales to weigh each piece – it should be around 50–60g (2–3oz). Arrange the rolls on the lined baking trays with about 2.5cm (1in) between each roll. Cover the trays with damp tea-towels and leave somewhere warm for an hour, or until doubled in size.

Preheat your oven to 180°C (350°F) and place an empty baking tray on the bottom shelf.

Mix together the glaze ingredients, excluding the sesame seeds and salt, in a bowl. Uncover the rolls, brush with glaze and sprinkle over the sesame seeds and salt. Pour a cup of water into the empty baking tray inside the oven to create steam. Bake the rolls for 20 minutes, or until golden. Remove from the oven and transfer to a wire rack. Leave the oven on if you're making the "fish" now. (Store cooled buns in sealed plastic sandwich bags if not using straight away.)

For the "fish", line a baking tray with baking paper and, if it isn't already on, preheat your oven to 180°C (350°F). Arrange the tofu fingers on the tray, place the pieces of nori on top of each piece of tofu, then drizzle over the lemon juice and sprinkle over the salt.

Mix the chickpea flour in a bowl with enough of the water to make a sticky egg-like mixture. Put the breadcrumbs in another bowl.

Individually dip the tofu into the flour mixture, making sure each is well covered, then coat in the crumbs and place back onto the lined baking tray. Bake for 20 minutes, or until golden.

While the "fish" is baking, make the mayonnaise. I recommend using a hand stick blender. Blend the milk, vinegar and lemon juice together in a tall jug and, while still blending, gradually add the oil. Keep blending until you've added all the oil and the mixture is a creamy mayo-like consistency. Stir in seasoning and sriracha to taste. Once the "fish" is cooked, build your sliders and serve.

5-spice
PAN-ROASTED
MUSHROOM WRAPS
WITH HOISIN SAUCE

This is the ultimate party food – everyone helps themselves. Hoisin sauce has always been a favourite of mine and it's so simple to make. To save time you can use shop-bought 5-spice powder but there is something special about making it yourself. I love cooking mushrooms this way, 100% inspired by my friend and chef Derek Sarno who is king of mushrooms!

800g (28oz) mixed mushrooms,
4 tbsp groundnut oil, for frying
155g (1 cup) raw cashew nuts,
  toasted
½ a cucumber, cut into
  thin strips
1 carrot, peeled into ribbons
3 spring onions (scallions),
  cut into thin strips
3 tbsp mixed sesame seeds,
  to sprinkle
6 Chinese pancakes (or large lettuce
  leaves, if gluten-free)

FOR THE HOISIN SAUCE
1 tbsp tahini
4 tbsp soy sauce
2 tbsp dark brown sugar
½ tsp roasted garlic powder
1 tbsp sesame oil
2 tsp Sriracha
juice of ½ lime

FOR THE 5-SPICE
2 star anise
2 tsp ground cinnamon
5 cloves
2 tsp fennel seeds
½ tsp ground ginger

Makes
6 wraps

Cooks In
45 minutes

Difficulty
5/10

GFO
**If lettuce
wraps are used**

I like to use a mixture of bunashimeji, king oyster (eryngii), oyster, enoki and maitake mushrooms – packs of mixed mushrooms like these can be found at most supermarkets.

MUSHROOM WRAP RECIPE CONTINUED

First up, mix together all the ingredients for the hoisin sauce in a small mixing bowl and set aside.

Put all the 5-spice ingredients in a pestle and mortar and grind them until you have a fine powder. Alternatively put the ingredients in a spice blender and blitz until fine.

Trim off any roots from the mushrooms and brush off any dirt. Slice the king oysters lengthways as they are a lot bigger than the other mushrooms.

Now for the fun part: grab a large, heavy-based, non-stick frying pan, place it over a high heat and add the oil. When the pan is smoking add all of the mushrooms – it may look like it is overfilled now but they will shrink an awful lot.

Grab another frying pan, or a saucepan, that's slightly smaller than the mushroom pan and sit it directly on top of the mushrooms. This is a technique I picked up from a big inspiration of mine, Derek Sarno. It will flatten the mushrooms and make sure they are all being seared completely. Leave the mushrooms for 4 minutes to cook, char and flavour up. Remove the top pan and flip over the mushrooms. Place the pan back on top and cook for a further 4 minutes. Don't worry if the mushrooms are a little blackened – it will add incredible flavour.

Remove the top pan and stir in 1 tablespoon of the 5-spice mix and 2 tablespoons of the hoisin sauce. Place the small pan back on top, turn the heat down low and leave the mushrooms to cook for 12 minutes, stirring every now and then.

The mushrooms should be glazed and charred with lovely crispy bits. Spoon them out of the pan onto a chopping board and roughly chop them up.

Gently heat your wraps in a pan or toaster (or wash your lettuce leaves, if using). It's nice if you let your guests fill their own wraps – add plenty of hoisin sauce, mushrooms, cucumber, carrot and spring onions, then sprinkle sesame seeds on top.

Quiches

These have always been a family favourite, but I never thought we could have them again until I started experimenting. After a few attempts I found that a combination of tofu, soy cream and gram flour really works to create an egg-like consistency once baked. Feel free to use shop-bought vegan shortcrust pastry to save time.

FOR THE PASTRY
375g (3 cups) plain (all-purpose) flour, plus extra for dusting
pinch of salt
125g (1 cup) vegan spread
3 tbsp nutritional yeast (optional)
2 tbsp non-dairy milk

FOR THE QUICHE FILLING
390g (13¾oz) firm block tofu, all water removed
3 tbsp chickpea (gram) flour
180ml (¾ cup) soy/oat cream or milk
3 tbsp nutritional yeast (optional)
¼ tsp roasted garlic powder
¼ tsp turmeric
1 tbsp tahini
1 tsp sea salt
½ tsp ground pepper

FOR THE FLAVOURINGS
2 tbsp rapeseed oil
1 leek, finely chopped
2 garlic cloves, crushed
2 slices of "bacon" (see page 12), sliced into lardons (optional)
handful of pitted olives
2 handfuls of baby spinach
6 cherry tomatoes, halved

TO SERVE
handful of fresh rocket (arugula)

Makes
6 mini 10cm (4in) quiches or one 25cm (10in) quiche

Cooks In
70 minutes

Difficulty
7/10

GFO
If gluten-free pastry is used

First up, make the pastry: place all the ingredients except the milk in a large mixing bowl. Rub the margarine into the dry ingredients with your fingers until the mixture resembles breadcrumbs.

Pour in enough milk to bring the mixture together to form a dough and pick up all the bits from the bowl. Give it a slight knead for 2 minutes and that's it, pastry done. Wrap the dough in cling film (plastic wrap) and pop into the fridge to chill for 20 minutes or so before rolling out. You can also used shop-bought vegan shortcrust pastry (or a gluten-free equivalent).

Meanwhile, prepare the flavourings and preheat your oven to 180°C (350°F). Grease the individual 10cm (4in) tart pans or you can use a 25cm (10in) loose-bottomed tart pan. Remove the pastry from the fridge.

QUICHES RECIPE CONTINUED

Put all the quiche filling ingredients into a blender and blitz until smooth and creamy. Set aside.

Roll out your pastry on a sheet of lightly floured greaseproof paper to around 3mm (⅛in) thick and large enough to line all the pans. Carefully lift up the greaseproof paper and pastry, then turn it out over the tart pans making sure the pastry is covering the whole of each pan with some overhang. Carefully peel away the greaseproof paper, lightly flour your hands and gently press the pastry into the corners and indentations of the sides of the pans.

Cut away any overhanging pastry. Place circles of greaseproof paper into the pastry cases and fill with baking beans or rice. Place the pans onto a baking sheet and into the oven to blind bake for 10 minutes. After 10 minutes, remove the paper and baking beans, then place the sheet back into the oven to cook the pastry for a further 5 minutes, or until lightly golden.

Meanwhile, heat the rapeseed oil in a frying pan over a medium heat. Add the leek, garlic and "bacon" lardons, if using. Sauté for 4–5 minutes to soften, then tip into a mixing bowl with the olives and spinach. Add the creamy quiche mixture and fold together.

Once the pastry is cooked, remove from the oven, pour the quiche filling into the pastry cases and level the tops. Neatly arrange the halved cherry tomatoes on top.

Lower the oven temperature to 160°C (325°F) Place the filled quiches back into the oven on the bottom shelf to cook for 30–35 minutes, or until the filling has firmed up. Serve warm or cold with the rocket (arugula).

SMOKED CHILLI AND ROSEMARY DOUGH-BALL FONDUE

This is a showstopper – light fluffy dough balls flavoured with beautiful smoky chilli and rosemary. Simple to make, and – paired with my "cheese" sauce – they are divine.

FOR THE DOUGH BALLS
240ml (1 cup) lukewarm water
240ml (1 cup) lukewarm soy milk
2 tsp yeast
5 tbsp olive oil
500g (4 cups) strong white
 bread flour, plus extra for dusting
2 tsp sea salt
1 tbsp maple syrup
1 tbsp dried rosemary
1 tbsp smoked chilli flakes

FOR THE GLAZE
2 tbsp rapeseed oil
4 tbsp almond milk
4 tsp maple syrup or agave nectar

TOPPINGS
1 tbsp sea salt
1 tbsp dried garlic flakes
1 tbsp smoked chilli flakes
a few sprigs of fresh lemon thyme
 and rosemary, leaves picked

FOR THE "CHEESE" FONDUE
120g (½ cup) raw cashew nuts
120ml (½ cup) filtered cold water
120ml (½ cup) cold non-dairy milk
1 tbsp tapioca starch
3 tbsp nutritional yeast
1 tsp English mustard
1 tsp white miso
pinch of sea salt and white pepper
¼ tsp onion powder

Serves
10

Cooks In
180 minutes

Difficulty
5/10

First make the dough balls: mix the lukewarm water and milk with the yeast and olive oil, and leave it for around 10 minutes until slightly bubbly.

Combine the flour, salt, maple syrup, rosemary and chilli flakes in a large mixing bowl. Make a well in the middle, add the water and yeast mixture and stir until the mixture starts to form a dough.

Use your hands to form the dough, then tip it out onto a lightly floured work surface. Now it's time to knead. Knead the dough for around 8 minutes, when the dough should

DOUGH-BALL FONDUE RECIPE CONTINUED

be smooth and quite elastic. Add minimal flour while kneading, if required. Lightly oil the bowl and put the dough back in, place a clean damp tea-towel over the top of the bowl and leave somewhere warm for around 1 hour, or until it has doubled in size.

After an hour, remove the dough from the bowl, knock the dough back and knead for 3 minutes.

Line a baking tray with greaseproof paper and place a lightly greased ramekin in the middle. This will eventually be the place for your "cheese" sauce/fondue to sit.

Cut the dough into approximately 25 even pieces – each piece should be about 35g (1¼oz). Use kitchen scales to weigh them. Roll each piece into a ball: the best way to do this is by putting one hand on top of the dough ball on the work surface, press down slightly and move your hand in a circular motion.

Neatly place the balls around the ramekin as you go. Once you've rolled all the balls, place the damp tea-towel over the top and leave them somewhere warm to double in size. This should take around 30 minutes.

Preheat your oven to 200°C (400°F). Mix together the ingredients for the glaze in a small bowl and prepare the toppings.

When the dough balls have risen, use a pastry brush to brush some glaze over each one and sprinkle over the toppings. Bake in the preheated oven for 30 minutes on the bottom shelf.

While the dough balls are baking, make the "cheese" sauce/fondue. Soak the cashew nuts for around 10 minutes in boiling water, then drain away the water and add the softened nuts to a high- speed blender with all the other ingredients. Blend on full speed until you have a smooth mixture.

Pour the mixture into a non-stick saucepan and stir with a spatula over a medium heat. Be patient – you will be stirring for around 8 minutes. Stir until it has thickened but is still pourable.

Remove the dough balls from the oven and let them cool slightly. When they're cool enough to handle, pour the "cheese" sauce into the ramekin in the middle of the tray, sprinkle over a few extra chilli flakes, and serve.

CENTRE
pieces

"NO-TURKEY"
WRAPPED IN GAZ'S STREAKY "BACON"

This is technical to make but so rewarding when you slice into it. I believe this recipe is powerful enough to help reduce the amount of people having meat on their dinner tables at Christmas – the flavours are incredible!

FOR THE "TURKEY"
WET INGREDIENTS
240ml (1 cup) soy or oat milk
10g (½ cup) dried mushrooms
olive oil, for frying
1 onion, finely chopped,
 sautéed until soft
3 garlic cloves, finely chopped,
 sautéed until soft
120ml (½ cup) white wine
50g (¼ cup) tinned chickpeas
 (garbanzos), drained
 and rinsed
110g (4oz) firm tofu, patted dry
3 tbsp white miso paste
2 tsp maple syrup
1 tbsp dried tarragon
1 tbsp dried thyme
2 tsp dried rosemary
1 tsp dried sage
1 tsp cayenne pepper
2 tsp sea salt
1 tbsp cracked black pepper

DRY INGREDIENTS
300g (2¾ cups) vital wheat gluten
50g (½ cup) chickpea (gram) flour
2 tbsp nutritional yeast

FOR THE BROTH
960ml (4 cups) vegetable stock
480ml (2 cups) white wine
2 sprigs of fresh rosemary
2 sprigs of fresh thyme
1 onion, quartered
handful of dried mushrooms
1 bay leaf
3 garlic cloves, peeled
pinch of sea salt and pepper

FOR THE RUB
4 tbsp mixed dried herbs
1 tsp cayenne pepper
½ tsp onion salt

FOR THE STUFFING
1 quantity Sweet potato and chestnut
 stuffing (page 116), skipping the
 final step

FOR THE "BACON" WRAPPING
3 tbsp Cranberry and orange sauce
 (page 112)
8 slices of Streaky "bacon" (page 12)
3 tbsp maple syrup

Serves
8

Cooks In
120 minutes

Difficulty
7/10

If you have a soy allergy, use 50g
(1¾oz) extra chickpeas instead of the tofu.
Use soy-free miso, or leave it out.

STUFFED "NO TURKEY" RECIPE CONTINUED

First up, you will need to make the seitan "turkey": combine all the wet ingredients in a blender and blend until smooth.

Mix the vital wheat gluten, chickpea flour and nutritional yeast together in a large mixing bowl or a stand mixer (with the dough hook attached), then add the wet ingredients and mix until it forms a dough.

Tip the dough onto a clean work surface and knead for at least 10 minutes by hand or do this in your mixer on medium speed. This is the most important part of the recipe – if you don't knead it properly you will be left with horrible spongy seitan. Be very firm!

Once kneaded, the dough should be quite firm and elastic. Use a rolling pin to bash and roll the dough into a rough rectangle around 1.25cm (½in) thick. Set the dough aside to rest for 10 minutes.

Add the broth ingredients to a large roasting tray, around 40 x 28 x 8cm (16 x 11 x 3in). Cut a piece of muslin (cheesecloth) slightly larger than the seitan dough rectangle.

Mix the rub ingredients together in a small bowl, then sprinkle it over the dough. Cover the seitan well in the spice mix as this stops it sticking. Place the dough spice-side down onto the muslin.

Spoon the stuffing across the middle of the dough and roll it up around the stuffing, moulding the edges together. Wrap the dough in the muslin as tightly as possible. Twist the ends, then tie them tightly with cook's string. Make sure your dough is a nice cylindrical shape.

Place the "No-Turkey" wrap into the roasting tray with the broth ingredients then cover the tray with foil. Place the tray into the oven for 2 hours. Turn the seitan over halfway through cooking and add additional stock if needed. Once cooked, use a slotted spoon to lift the "turkey" out of the broth and, when cool enough to handle, carefully remove the muslin. The "turkey" can now be wrapped in clingfilm and placed into the fridge until you're ready to serve it. Reserve the broth liquid as it makes a great gravy.

An hour before you want to serve, preheat your oven to 180°C (350°F). I like to wrap the "turkey" in my "bacon" but you can bake it without if you prefer. Place the "turkey" into a baking tray, spoon over a couple of tablespoons of cranberry sauce to help the "bacon" stick, then neatly lay over the rashers. Secure it with string, if necessary. Brush with the maple syrup to glaze. Bake for 25 minutes, then slice and serve with all the trimmings!

RICH WHITE WINE GRAVY

Packed full of umami flavour, this gravy goes well with all of the centre pieces in the book.

2 carrots, peeled
2 red onions, peeled
250g (9oz) chestnut mushrooms
2 garlic cloves
1 leek
2 celery sticks
1 tbsp olive oil
pinch of sea salt and pepper
2 tbsp plain (all-purpose) flour
 (or gluten-free flour)

240ml (1 cup) vegan-friendly
 white wine
1 tbsp soy sauce
1 tbsp white miso paste
juice of 1 lemon
1 tbsp dried tarragon
2 sprigs of fresh thyme
2 sprigs of fresh sage
1 sprig of fresh rosemary
480ml (2 cups) vegetable stock

Serves
6

Cooks In
35 minutes

Difficulty
2/10

GF
**If gluten-free
flour is used**

Roughly chop the carrots, onions, mushrooms, garlic, leek and celery.

Heat the olive oil in a large saucepan over a medium heat. When the pan is hot, add the onions and mushrooms and sauté for 2 minutes until they've shrunk in size. Add the rest of the chopped vegetables and a pinch of seasoning and continue to sauté for 3 minutes, stirring often, until they caramelize but make sure they don't burn. Stir in the flour and cook for 1 more minute.

Pour in the white wine and stir to deglaze the pan, then lower the heat. Add the soy sauce, miso paste and lemon juice, followed by the herbs. Cook for 2 minutes to allow the flavours to intensify, then add the vegetable stock. It's now time to leave the gravy to simmer and reduce down for 20 minutes.

The gravy should now be a lot thicker. Pour it through a fine sieve into a smaller saucepan, pressing with the back of a ladle to get as much of the liquid goodness out of the vegetables as possible. If the gravy is thinner than you'd like, simmer for a few more minutes for it to reduce some more.

Serve the gravy straight away or store in a sealed container in the fridge for up to 3 days, then reheat in a saucepan.

Stuffed SQUASH ROAST

What a beautiful array of flavours and colours,
all stuffed inside my favourite vegetable.

1 large butternut squash, washed
a little olive oil

FOR THE GLAZED ONIONS
2 red onions, finely sliced
3 tbsp balsamic vinegar
5 tbsp organic coconut sugar

FOR THE CHRISTMAS RICE
150g (¾ cup) wild rice, cooked
150g (5½oz) whole cooked vacuum-
 packed chestnuts, roughly chopped
75g (2½oz) dried apricots, chopped
150g (1 cup) mixed nuts, chopped
pinch of cayenne pepper
pinch of paprika

juice of ½ lemon
pinch of sea salt and pepper
pinch of dried sage

FOR THE SAUTÉED MUSHROOMS
160g (1½ cups) fresh mushrooms
 (I used girolles)
1 tsp roasted garlic powder
sea salt and pepper
5 tbsp Cranberry and orange sauce
 (see page 112)
4 peppers, roasted, skin removed
6 sun-dried tomatoes, re-hydrated
2 handfuls baby spinach

Serves
6

Cooks In
70 minutes

Difficulty
5/10

GF

Preheat your oven to 180°C (350°F). Split the squash in half lengthways, place cut-side up onto a baking tray and bake for 45 minutes, or until just soft.

Meanwhile, make the glazed onions. Heat 3 tablespoons of water in a non-stick sauce-pan, add the sliced onion and sweat for 5 minutes. Add the vinegar and sugar, then cook for a further 10 minutes over a low heat, stirring occasionally, until caramelized. Set aside.

Mix the Christmas rice ingredients in a mixing bowl until fully combined, then set aside.

Sauté your mushrooms. Heat 2 tablespoons of water in a non-stick frying pan over a medium heat. Add the mushrooms, garlic powder and seasoning. Sauté for 5 minutes.

When the squash is cooked and cooled slightly, scoop out the seeds, then scoop out a 2cm (1in) channel of flesh and mix that into the Christmas rice mixture. Spoon the cranberry sauce into one of the squash halves, followed by the rice. Top with the peppers, onions, mushrooms, sun-dried tomatoes and spinach. Place the other squash half on top, tie to-gether in three places and roast for a further 15 minutes. Carve and serve straight away.

The
ULTIMATE
Christmas
R~O~A~S~T

This is Christmas, all wrapped up ... literally! The Christmassy flavours we all
love are in this roast "beef" wellington. It's so succulent and flavoursome.

FOR THE "BEEF"

WET INGREDIENTS
2 tbsp vegetable oil
1 onion, finely chopped
1 leek, finely chopped
2 garlic cloves, crushed
1 tsp sea salt
1 tsp cracked black pepper
pinch of cinnamon
pinch of allspice
pinch of paprika
pinch of ground nutmeg
1 tbsp dried sage
2 tsp dried rosemary
30g (¼ cup) dried cranberries
50g (½ cup) dried apricots
100g (1 cup) peeled and cooked
　chestnuts
240ml (1 cup) cider, from a
　500ml (2 cup) bottle
240ml (1 cup) vegetable stock
1 tbsp miso paste

DRY INGREDIENTS
250g (2¼ cups) vital wheat gluten
3 tbsp chickpea (gram) flour

FOR THE SPICE RUB
1 tsp cayenne
1 tsp allspice
1 tsp dried sage
1 tsp dried rosemary
1 tsp dried tarragon

FOR ROASTING
remaining 260ml (1 cup) cider
1 orange
500ml (2 cups) vegetable stock
1 onion
2 garlic cloves
1 bay leaf
handful of fresh thyme and rosemary
　sprigs
1 tbsp miso paste
2 tbsp balsamic vinegar

4 tbsp Cranberry and orange sauce
　(page 112)
320g (11¼oz) block ready-made
　vegan puff pastry

FOR THE GLAZE
3 tbsp maple syrup
3 tbsp non-dairy milk
4 tbsp vegetable oil

FOR THE GRAVY
2 tbsp cornflour (cornstarch)
4 tbsp water

Serves
6

Cooks In
150 minutes

Difficulty
7/10

THE ULTIMATE CHRISTMAS ROAST RECIPE CONTINUED

Make the "meat" dough. Heat the oil a non-stick frying pan over a medium heat. Fry the onion, leek, garlic, seasoning, spices and herbs for 2–3 minutes.

Meanwhile put the cranberries, apricots and chestnuts into a blender and blitz until they're all a similar size. Add these to the frying pan and sauté for 3–4 minutes until everything has softened. Pour in the cider, stock and miso paste. Stir together and allow the mixture to simmer for 2 minutes before turning the heat off.

Combine the dry ingredients. Once the wet mixture has cooled slightly, mix with the dry ingredients. It should form a nice dough. If your mix is wet add a little more chickpea flour. Tip the dough out onto a clean work surface and knead for 10 minutes. Leave to rest.

Preheat your oven to 170°C (340°F). Combine the rub spices in a bowl. Shape the dough into a sausage 10cm (4in) in diameter. Sprinkle the rub onto your work surface. Roll the dough in the rub.

Roll the dough in a piece of muslin (cheesecloth), twist the ends tightly, then tie each end with cook's string to secure it. Place the wrapped dough into a deep baking tray together with the rest of the roasting ingredients and bake for 2 hours on the bottom shelf, turning over half way through to ensure it cooks evenly. Once baked, lift the roast out of the tray, reserving the roasting liquid, leave to cool slightly, then remove the muslin. At this point you can either chill it in the fridge for up to 3 days or continue. If you are not cooking now, make the gravy (below) and keep in the fridge, then reheat.

An hour before you want to serve, roll out your pastry into a tea-towel-sized rectangle around 3mm (⅛in) thick. Cut strips a third of the width of the pastry on each side, so you can cross them to make a lattice. Spread the cranberry and orange sauce over the roast, lift it into the centre of the pastry, wrap it up, then transfer to a baking sheet lined with non-stick baking paper. Combine the glaze ingredients in a bowl, then brush over the top of the pastry. Bake for 15–20 minutes, or until golden.

While the wellington is cooking, strain the roasting liquid from the baking tray through a sieve into a saucepan, pressing to squeeze out all the lovely juices. Place over a low heat and simmer for 10 minutes until you have a thick gravy. Mix the cornflour with the water and add it to the gravy whilst whisking until it thickens to your desired consistency. Remove the wellington from the oven, carve and serve with the rich gravy.

ROSEMARY, RED WINE AND GARLIC
"BEEF"
with Rich Jus

Packed with hearty flavours, this seitan "beef" roast is seriously good.
The broth reduces down to create the ultimate jus. You can make the "beef"
up to three days in advance of serving, providing you store it in the fridge.

FOR THE "BEEF"
WET INGREDIENTS
160ml (⅔ cup) hot vegetable stock
10g (½ cup) dried porcini
olive oil, for frying
1 red onion, finely chopped
3 garlic cloves, finely chopped
120ml (½ cup) red wine
50g (¼ cup) chopped cooked
 beetroot (beet)
50g (½ cup) tinned black beans,
 drained and rinsed
2 tbsp tomato purée (paste)
1 tbsp Dijon mustard
2 tbsp balsamic vinegar
1 tbsp miso paste
2 tsp Marmite
3 tsp dried mixed herbs
1 tsp cayenne pepper
3 tsp dried rosemary
2 tsp sea salt
1 tbsp cracked black pepper

DRY INGREDIENTS
300g (2¾ cups) vital wheat gluten
50g (½ cup) chickpea (gram) flour,
 plus extra for dusting
2 tbsp nutritional yeast

FOR THE BROTH
720ml (3 cups) vegetable stock
480ml (2 cups) red wine
1 tbsp miso paste
1 onion, peeled and quartered
3 garlic cloves, peeled
1 bay leaf
3 sprigs of fresh rosemary
4 tbsp dried mushrooms
2 tsp cornflour (cornstarch), optional
1 tbsp Cranberry and orange sauce
 (page 112)

FOR THE HERB COATING
¼ tsp dried sage
¼ tsp dried oregano
¼ tsp cayenne pepper
¼ tsp dried rosemary
¼ tsp dried tarragon
1 tbsp cracked black pepper

FOR ROASTING
2 tbsp wholegrain mustard
2 tsp cracked black pepper
2 tbsp smoked olive oil (or olive oil)

TO SERVE
sprig of fresh rosemary
sea salt flakes

Serves
8–10

Cooks In
120 minutes

Difficulty
7/10

"BEEF" RECIPE CONTINUED

First make the "beef". Pour the hot vegetable stock over the porcini in a small bowl and set aside for 5 minutes for the porcini to rehydrate.

Heat a splash of olive oil in a non-stick saucepan. Add the onion and garlic, reduce the heat and allow them to soften for 2 minutes, stirring often. Remove from the heat and tip them into a blender with the remaining wet ingredients, plus the mushrooms and stock. Let the mixture cool for 5 minutes before you blitz. This gives you time to prep the dry ingredients – combine them in a large bowl.

Blitz the wet ingredients together until smooth, then pour into the mixing bowl of dry ingredients and quickly stir with a spatula until everything is well combined into a dough.

Using an electric stand mixer with a dough hook, knead on medium speed for 10 minutes. If hand kneading, knead the dough on your work surface for 12 minutes. Add a sprinkle of additional chickpea (gram) flour to stop it from sticking. Return the dough to the bowl and cover with a clean tea-towel to rest and firm up for 15 minutes.

Meanwhile, heat all the broth ingredients, except the cranberry sauce, in a saucepan, bring to the boil, then reduce to simmering.

Shape the dough into a rough fillet shape to make it easier for wrapping in pastry. Mix the herb coating ingredients together, then sprinkle it onto your work surface and roll the fillet in it.

Wrap the fillet in muslin (cheesecloth) and tie the ends with cook's string – this holds the shape. Lower the fillet into the simmering broth, pop the lid on and cook for 1 hour 15 minutes until firm to touch. Make sure the broth is simmering, never boiling. Carefully turn the fillet over a couple of times so that it cooks evenly. Once cooked, remove from the broth and, when cool enough, remove the muslin.

Strain the broth into a saucepan. Heat gently until it has reduced and thickened to form a jus. Add a little cornflour (cornstarch) blended with cold water if it's not thickening. Stir in the cranberry sauce for a touch of sweetness.

One hour before serving, preheat your oven to 180°C (350°F). Spread the mustard over the fillet and sprinkle over the black pepper. Heat a large ovenproof pan on a high heat, add the oil and brown the fillet on all sides. Transfer the pan to the oven and roast for 15–20 minutes. Top with a sprig of fresh rosemary and a sprinkle of sea salt. Slice into thick pieces and serve with the jus in a jug ready for pouring.

INDULGENT VEGAN CHRISTMAS

AUBERGINE PLATTER

A lighter option for your Christmas spread, but no compromise on taste. Make sure you char the aubergines before baking – it adds loads of flavour.

4 aubergines (eggplants), cut in half lengthways
1 tbsp miso paste
2 tbsp maple syrup
3 tbsp rapeseed oil

FOR THE STUFFING
1 tbsp rapeseed oil
1 red onion, cubed
1 garlic clove, crushed
1 red (bell) pepper, cubed
1 courgette (zucchini), cubed
1 sprig of fresh rosemary, leaves picked, finely chopped
1 tbsp fresh thyme leaves
¼ tsp ground cinnamon
¼ tsp ground allspice
½ tsp cayenne
zest of 1 orange
4 tomatoes, cubed

225g (1½ cups) quinoa or couscous, cooked
4 tbsp pine nuts
1 tsp sea salt
1 tsp black pepper

FOR THE TAHINI DRESSING
3 tbsp tahini
120ml (½ cup) cold water
juice of ½ lemon
pinch of sea salt and pepper

FOR THE PARSNIP CRISP (OPTIONAL)
1 parsnip, peeled
3 tbsp vegetable oil
pinch of sea salt and pepper

TO SERVE
fresh thyme leaves
seeds of ½ pomegranate
handful of walnuts, toasted

Serves
4

Cooks In
60 minutes

Difficulty
2/10

GF

Line a baking tray with non-stick baking paper and preheat your oven to 180°C (350°F).

In a small mixing bowl, whisk together the miso, maple syrup and 2 tablespoons of the oil with a fork or small whisk until smooth.

Heat a griddle pan and add the remaining oil. When the pan is very hot, add the aubergines, cut-side down (do this in batches if your pan is small). Char the aubergines for around 3 minutes on both sides, transferring to the lined baking tray, cut-side up, as you go.

STUFFED AUBERGINE PLATTER RECIPE CONTINUED

Generously spread the miso mix over the top of the aubergines, then pop them into the oven to cook through for 10 minutes.

Meanwhile make the stuffing. Heat the oil in a large non-stick frying pan over a medium heat. Add the onion, garlic, pepper and courgette and fry, stirring, for 2 minutes before adding the herbs, spices and orange zest. Cook for 4–5 minutes more, until softened. Stir in the tomatoes, quinoa, pine nuts and seasoning, then turn off the heat.

Remove the aubergines from the oven. Carefully (as they are very hot) use a fork to squish down the flesh in the centre of the aubergines leaving a 1cm (½in) border all around the edge. (I much prefer doing it this way as I don't want to lose any of the flavour which could happen if you scoop the filling out the traditional way.)

Spoon the vegetable stuffing mix generously into the aubergines, then place them back into the oven for a further 15 minutes.

If you are serving your stuffed aubergines with crispy parsnips, make them now. Use a swivel peeler to peel the parsnip flesh into ribbons. Add them to a bowl and pour over the oil. Sprinkle with seasoning and give it a good mix, making sure all the ribbons are well coated.

Line a baking tray with greaseproof paper and spread out the parsnip ribbons. You don't have to be overly neat just make sure they aren't all on top of one another. Bake in the oven on the middle shelf for 10–12 minutes. Alternatively, for extra crispy parsnips, you can shallow fry them. Heat your oil to around 180°C (350°F), then carefully place the parsnip ribbons into the oil to fry for 3–4 minutes, or until golden. Remove the ribbons from the oil using a slotted spoon and place them onto a plate lined with kitchen paper. The parsnips will crisp up after a couple minutes of cooling.

Just before serving, mix together all the ingredients for the tahini dressing with a fork in a small mixing bowl. Check the seasoning before serving.

When the aubergines are ready, arrange them on a serving platter, generously topped with tahini dressing, crispy parsnips, fresh thyme, pomegranate seeds and toasted walnuts.

Festive Nut
ROAST
WREATH

Well, it wouldn't be a vegan Christmas without a nut roast!
Roasted in a wreath tin and topped with my cranberry sauce,
it's the perfect Christmas centre piece.

3 tbsp olive oil
1 red onion, finely chopped
1 celery stick, finely chopped
2 garlic cloves, chopped
1 leek, finely chopped
200g (7oz) butternut squash, peeled, and cut into small cubes
1 small aubergine (eggplant), cut into small cubes
60g (2oz) vacuum-packed chestnuts, roughly chopped
½ tsp allspice
¼ tsp ground cinnamon
1 sprig of fresh rosemary, finely chopped
10 fresh sage leaves, finely chopped
sea salt and pepper
1 orange, zest and juice
140g (1 cup) mixed nuts (Brazil nuts, pistachios, walnuts, etc.)
165g (1 cup) cooked chickpeas (garbanzos)

45g (½ cup) gluten-free breadcrumbs
50g (⅓ cup) dried cranberries, roughly chopped
50g (¼ cup) dried apricots, roughly chopped
50g (⅓ cup) sun-dried tomatoes, roughly chopped
3 tbsp balsamic vinegar
1 tbsp white miso paste
3 tbsp nutritional yeast
1 tbsp Marmite

FOR THE CRANBERRY TOPPING
6 tbsp Cranberry and orange sauce (page 112)

OPTIONAL GARNISHES
fried sage leaves (page 117)
shelled pistachios
dried oranges
fresh rosemary

Serves
6

Cooks In
70 minutes

Difficulty
5/10

GF

FESTIVE NUT ROAST WREATH RECIPE CONTINUED

Preheat your oven to 180°C (350°F). Grease a non-stick 25cm (10in) cake ring mould/tin. (Line with baking paper if it's not non-stick.)

Heat the olive oil in a large saucepan over a medium heat and sauté the onion, celery, garlic, leek, squash, aubergine and chestnuts for a few minutes, stirring frequently. Add the spices, herbs, some seasoning and the orange zest. Turn the heat down and cook for 8–10 minutes, stirring every now and then. You want all the flavours to marry together and the vegetables to soften slightly.

While the vegetables are cooking, blitz the nuts in a blender until they are a crumb-like consistency. Add the chickpeas and pulse it a couple times just to break them down slightly. Tip these into the saucepan and add the breadcrumbs, cranberries, apricots and sun-dried tomatoes, stirring well.

Add the vinegar, miso paste, nutritional yeast and Marmite and cook for 3–4 minutes, stirring often, then turn off the heat.

Spoon the Cranberry and orange sauce into the tin and spread out evenly, then carefully spread the nut roast mixture on top. Press the mix into the tin as much as you can. Once you've filled the tin, cover it over with foil and roast in the preheated oven for 30–35 minutes.

After roasting, allow to cool slightly before turning out of the tin. Serve your festive nut roast wreath topped with your chosen garnishes.

Rich
MUSHROOM
AND LENTIL PARCELS

These are delicious, with hearty lentils and meaty portobello mushrooms.
I usually make the rich filling the day before, to let the flavours deepen.

3 tbsp rapeseed oil
1 onion, very finely chopped
2 garlic cloves, crushed
1 celery stick, very finely chopped
1 carrot, peeled and very finely
  chopped
5 portobello mushrooms,
  cleaned, trimmed and cut into
  1cm (½in) cubes
2 tsp cracked black pepper
4 tbsp plain (all-purpose) flour
240ml (1 cup) vegan-friendly
  red wine
720ml (3 cups) vegetable stock
300g (1½ cups) puy lentils, rinsed
2 tbsp soy sauce (or coconut aminos)

1 tbsp Marmite or miso paste
2 tbsp fresh thyme leaves
1 tbsp fresh rosemary leaves, finely
  chopped
1 tbsp dried tarragon
1 bay leaf
1 tsp dried sage
1 tbsp redcurrant jelly (or Cranberry
  and orange sauce, see page 112)
2 x 270g (9½oz) packs filo pastry
flour, for dusting

FOR THE GLAZE
60ml (¼ cup) non-dairy milk
4 tbsp maple syrup
4 tbsp oil

Makes
8–10 parcels

Cooks In
60 minutes

Difficulty
7/10

First up, make the rich filling. Heat the oil in a large lidded saucepan over a medium
heat. When it's hot, add the onion, garlic, celery and carrot and sauté for 3 minutes, or
until soft and golden. Add the mushrooms, stirring well, and cook for a good 5 minutes
to remove the excess water and colour, nicely which will give the filling a great depth of
flavour. Add a pinch of the cracked black pepper, then stir in the flour. Lower the heat
and stir for 2–3 minutes for the flour to cook.

Pour in the red wine and stock, stir well and scrape any bits off the bottom of the pan
using your spoon. Add the lentils, soy sauce, Marmite, herbs and redcurrant jelly and
the remaining pepper. Give everything a good stir, pop the lid on and leave to cook for

MUSHROOM AND LENTIL PARCEL RECIPE CONTINUED

15–20 minutes. Stir every now and then and if it gets too thick add a touch more stock.

Once the lentils are tender, taste the mixture and add seasoning if needed. When you're happy, scrape the mixture into a deep tray, lined with baking paper, and allow to cool completely. Ideally, chill in the fridge overnight.

Two hours before serving, preheat your oven to 180°C (350°F) and line a baking tray with non-stick baking paper. Mix together your glaze ingredients in a small bowl and grab a pastry brush.

Unroll your filo pastry and place one sheet on a lightly floured surface. Brush with glaze, then spoon 4 tablespoons of the filling towards the bottom of the sheet, leaving a 5cm (2in) border. Fold over the borders then simply roll up. Brush the parcel with additional glaze then transfer it to the lined baking tray. Repeat until you've used up all the filling and made six parcels.

Bake the parcels in the oven for 25 minutes, or until golden and crisp. Serve straight away with Grilled tenderstem (page 110), Celeriac purée (page 111), Orange-glazed carrots (page 104) and gravy (page 67).

Shallot
TARTE TATIN

Unveil this tarte tatin to your guests and you will be worshipped!

4 tbsp rapeseed oil
5–6 banana shallots, peeled, cut
in half lengthways, roots trimmed
3 tbsp soft brown sugar
4 tbsp balsamic vinegar
2 tbsp vegan-friendly brandy
(optional)
2 sprigs of fresh thyme

1 sprig of fresh rosemary
½ tsp sea salt
½ tsp cracked black pepper
320g (11¼oz) ready made vegan
puff pastry
plain (all-purpose) flour, for rolling

Serves
4

Cooks In
60 minutes

Difficulty
7/10

GFO
**If gluten-free
pastry is used**

Preheat your oven to 170°C (340°F). Roll out the pastry on a lightly floured surface to around 4mm (⅙in) thick, then cut it into a circle about 2.5cm (1in) wider than your pan.

Heat your ovenproof, heavy-based frying pan over a medium heat and heat 3 tablespoons of the oil. Add the shallots, cut-side up, making sure you have enough to fill the base. Cook for 3–4 minutes, then sprinkle over the brown sugar. Flip over the shallots using a palette knife – arrange them neatly, so that the base is covered and there aren't any gaps.

Turn the heat down low, then add the balsamic vinegar and brandy, if using. (Allow the alcohol to cook off, leaving behind the sweet brandy flavour.) Add the leaves from one sprig of thyme and the rosemary and let the onions caramelize for 4–5 minutes. Sprinkle over the salt and pepper, then turn off the heat and drizzle the remaining oil on the top.

Carefully lift your pastry and lay it over the pan. Quickly and carefully tuck the pastry down right into the edges using a wooden spoon so you don't have to touch the hot pan, then pop into the oven to bake for 25–30 minutes, or until the pastry is lovely and golden.

Once cooked, remove the tart from the oven and allow it to cool for 2–3 minutes. Place a plate on top of the pan (make sure it's larger than the pan!), wear an oven glove to protect the arm holding the board (some caramel goodness may drip out and it's super-hot), then quickly, carefully and confidently flip the pan and board/plate to turn it out.

Serve straight away. This tart tastes amazing with Truffle cream "cheese" (page 156) and the remaining fresh thyme.

NO PIGS
in Blankets

Just look at these! You should have seen the expression on my face when
I cracked this recipe. This just proves there really is no need to eat animals.
Any oil will do if you don't have smoked olive oil.

FOR THE SAUSAGES
16 mini sausages (page 42)

FOR THE "BACON"
16 rashers of Streaky "bacon"
(page 12)
3 tbsp smoked olive oil
3 tbsp maple syrup

Makes
16

Cooks In
40 minutes

Difficulty
5/10

Preheat your oven to 170°C (340°F) and line a baking tray with non-stick baking paper.

Wrap each mini sausage in a slice of "bacon" and arrange the wrapped sausages on the
lined baking tray leaving space between each one.

Drizzle over the oil, brush with maple syrup, then cook the in the preheated oven for
25 minutes.

Serve straight away (but they are also good eaten cold the next day).

Use the sausage recipe on page 42 –
make them half the size and roll
them thinner.

HERB-CRUSTED

CAULIFLOWER
and Leek "Cheese"

This is creamy and cheesy, thanks to the coconut milk, miso and nutritional yeast. Of course, being a Welshman, I like to add leek as well. The herby breadcrumbs on top add a lovely crunch.

1 cauliflower, cut into florets
1 leek, sliced into 2cm (¾in) rounds

FOR THE "CHEESE" SAUCE
400ml (14fl oz) tin coconut milk
5 tbsp nutritional yeast
80g (½ cup) raw cashew nuts,
  soaked in water
1 shallot
1 tbsp white miso paste
6 tbsp non-dairy milk
juice of ½ lemon

pinch of sea salt and pepper
1 garlic clove
1 bay leaf
2 sprigs of fresh thyme

FOR THE HERB COATING
100g (1 cup) breadcrumbs
handful of fresh parsley
2 sprigs of fresh rosemary
handful of fresh sage leaves
4 sprigs of fresh thyme
3 tbsp rapeseed oil

Serves
4

Cooks In
40 minutes

Difficulty
2/10

GFO
If gluten-free breadcrumbs are used

First up, preheat the oven to 170°C (340°F) and heat a large saucepan of water until boiling. Add the cauliflower florets and leek slices and blanch for 3 minutes.

Meanwhile, put all the sauce ingredients, except the bay leaf and thyme, into a blender and blitz until smooth.

Lift out the cauliflower and leek with a slotted spoon into a bowl and set aside. Discard the water, place the pan back on a low heat and pour in the blended sauce. Add the bay leaf and thyme.

Clean out the blender and quickly blitz together the herb coating ingredients until you have fine crumbs.

Add the cauliflower and leek to the hot sauce, stir to combine everything, then tip the mixture into a 15 x 23cm (6 x 9in) ovenproof baking dish. Sprinkle over the herby breadcrumbs. Bake on the bottom shelf of the oven for 20 minutes, or until the topping is golden brown. Keep an eye on it – you don't want it to burn. Serve straight away.

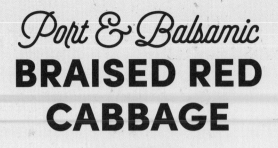

Port & Balsamic
BRAISED RED CABBAGE

Rich and indulgent, this cabbage has always been one of my favourite Christmas sides, while the apples add a lovely sweetness and the aromatic star anise adds a magic aniseed flavour.

2 tbsp rapeseed oil or water
1 red onion, finely sliced
1 red cabbage, finely shredded
2 crisp sweet apples, grated
 (Braeburns are ideal)
120ml (½ cup) vegan-friendly port
60ml (¼ cup) balsamic vinegar
zest and juice of 1 orange

100g (½ cup) soft brown
 or coconut sugar
1 star anise
1 cinnamon stick
1 tsp sea salt
2 tsp cracked black pepper
2 tbsp fresh thyme leaves, plus extra
 to garnish

Serves
6

Cooks In
60 minutes

Difficulty
2/10

GF

Heat the oil or water in a large, heavy-based, non-stick saucepan over a medium heat. Add the onion and sweat for 2–3 minutes, until soft and lightly golden.

Add the red cabbage and grated apple, turn the heat up and sauté for 3–4 minutes, stirring constantly.

The red cabbage will reduce in volume as it cooks – when it's half the original volume, turn the heat down low and pour in the port to deglaze the pan. Cook for a couple of minutes before adding the rest of the ingredients. Stir well, pop the lid on and leave the cabbage to cook for 55–60 minutes. Stir every now and then so it doesn't catch.

After an hour, the red cabbage should be tender and the liquid thickened to a glaze-like consistency. Sprinkle over a little extra fresh thyme before serving.

Photograph on **page 101**.

Sticky
BEETROOT
WITH WALNUTS

Liven up earthy beets by adding maple and orange, it caramelizes whilst cooking in the oven, creating lovely sticky glaze. I used a red beetroot, two candy striped (chioggia) and one golden.

4 medium-sized mixed
  beetroots (beets)
3 tbsp rapeseed oil or water
juice of ½ orange
3 tbsp maple syrup
2 tbsp balsamic vinegar
2 tbsp soy sauce or tamari
1 tsp cracked black pepper
100g (1 cup) walnut halves

Serves
4

Cooks In
60 minutes

Difficulty
2/10

GF

Preheat the oven to 180°C (350°F) and prepare the beetroots – wash and cut each one into 6–8 wedges, about 2.5cm (1in) thick.

Place the beetroot wedges in a deep ovenproof dish and add all the other ingredients except the walnuts. Mix everything together with your hands.

Place the dish into the oven and roast for 30 minutes, then remove the dish, mix in the walnuts and return to the oven for a further 15 minutes, or until the beetroots are tender.

Photograph on **page 101**.

Sexy SPROUTS

Even if you're not usually a sprout lover, I promise you will love these. Topping them with my coconut "bacon" bits just takes them to the next level.

500g (1lb) Brussels sprouts, trimmed
2 tbsp rapeseed oil
200g (2 cups) vacuum-packed chestnuts, halved
1 tsp fennel seeds
handful of dried cranberries
zest of 1 lemon
pinch of sea salt and pepper

FOR THE COCONUT "BACON" BITS
100g (1 cup) coconut flakes
2 tbsp maple syrup
1 tbsp sweet smoked paprika
2 tbsp soy sauce
1 tbsp coconut oil

Serves
4

Cooks In
25 minutes

Difficulty
2/10

GF

Preheat the oven 180°C (350°F) and line a baking tray with non-stick baking paper.

First up, make the coconut "bacon" bits. Put all the ingredients in a mixing bowl and stir well to coat the coconut flakes. Spread them out evenly over the lined baking tray and bake for 10–15 minutes, or until golden and crisp. Stir the coconut on the tray a couple of times during cooking to avoid it burning (which it can easily do).

For the sprouts, bring a large saucepan of water to the boil. Gradually add the sprouts to the water, making sure the water keeps at a rolling boil, and cook until tender and a vibrant green colour, usually around 3–4 minutes. Once the sprouts are cooked, drain and place them onto a tray lined with kitchen paper to soak up excess water if cooking straight away. Alternatively, you can chill the sprouts in the fridge at this stage until you're ready to flavour them up just before serving.

Before serving, heat the rapeseed oil in a large work over a high heat. Add the sprouts and sauté them for 2 minutes, then add the rest of the ingredients and continue to cook over a high heat, stirring often, for 3 more minutes. A little colour on the sprouts adds great flavour.

Once your sprouts are nicely coloured, throw in a handful of coconut "bacon", saving the rest to sprinkle on top once you've dished up.

Gaz's
= BEST-EVER VEGAN =
ROASTIES

Crispy on the outside, fluffy on the inside... I love making (and eating!)
these. Shaking them in the pan roughs up the edges – vital for crispiness.

1kg (2.2lb) floury potatoes, such as
 Maris Piper, peeled
4 tbsp plain (all-purpose) flour
 (or a gluten-free flour)
4 tbsp rapeseed oil
4 tbsp coconut oil
1 tsp sea salt
1 tsp cracked black pepper
3 sprigs of fresh rosemary
3 shallots, peeled and quartered
4 garlic cloves

Serves
6

Cooks In
55 minutes

Difficulty
2/10

GFO
**If gluten-free
flour is used**

First up, preheat your oven to 180°C (350°F). Cut your potatoes into similar-sized
pieces, pop them into a large saucepan filled with water and add a pinch of salt.

Cover the saucepan and place it over a high heat. Bring to the boil and cook for
4–5 minutes, or until the potatoes just start to soften on the outsides.

Tip the parboiled potatoes into a colander to drain, then return them to the saucepan
to steam dry for a few minutes before sprinkling over the flour.

Place the lid back on the saucepan and give the pan a good shake for 30 seconds.
This creates the rough edges on the potatoes which is key to getting crispy roasties.

Pour the oils into a deep-sided, non-stick, metal baking tray and set on your hob over a
very low heat. Add the potatoes before it gets hot and allow the potatoes to colour a little
bit, turning them often, for around 3 minutes. Season the potatoes, and add the rosemary,
shallots and garlic to the tray.

Once the they are lightly golden, transfer the tray to the oven for 35 minutes, or until the
potatoes are crispy and golden. I usually turn my roasties half way through cooking.

Orange-glazed CARROTS

Jazz up your carrots by using orange juice – it helps them keep their
sweetness and colour as well as creating the most amazing glaze.
I like to use baby carrots for this dish.

300g (10½oz) carrots
480ml (2 cups) fresh orange juice
240ml (1 cup) vegetable stock
3 tbsp maple syrup
4 tbsp olive oil
handful of fresh thyme
1 tsp sea salt
1 tsp cracked black pepper
handful of pistachio nuts, to serve

Serves
6

Cooks In
20 minutes

Difficulty
2/10

GF

Peel your carrots if necessary and cut any large ones in half – make sure they're all a
similar size. I use baby carrots, so I scrub them clean with a scourer and split any large
ones lengthways.

Put the carrots in a large, lidded saucepan with the rest of the ingredients, cover and
place over a high heat. If squeezing your own juice, add one of the orange halves to
the pan for extra flavour. Cook the carrots until tender – baby carrots take around
8–10 minutes but it will depend on the size.

The orange sauce may have already reduced to a glaze-like consistency but if it hasn't,
lift the carrots out of the pan with a slotted spoon (keep on a plate) and continue to cook
until the liquid has reduced to a glaze. Once it has thickened, turn off the heat and return
the carrots to the pan. Toss them in the glaze a few times until they are coated, then serve
with pistachio nuts sprinkled over.

Maple PAN-ROASTED PARSNIPS

Pan-roasting the parsnips this way not only creates a beautiful flavour, but saves space in your oven on Christmas Day.

6 parsnips, peeled, cut into batons,
  fibrous centres removed
1 tsp sea salt
1 tsp ground white pepper
½ a lemon
3 tbsp rapeseed oil
4 tbsp maple syrup
3 sprigs of fresh thyme, leaves picked,
  plus extra for serving

Serves
6

Cooks In
25 minutes

Difficulty
2/10

GF

Place the parsnips into a saucepan and cover with water. Add a pinch of the seasoning, the thyme and the lemon half. Cover and place over a high heat.

Bring the parsnips to a boil and cook for 4–5 minutes, then drain into a colander. You can cook the parsnips until this point the day before serving and keep covered in the fridge overnight.

About 25 minutes before serving, heat the oil in a large, non-stick saucepan over a medium heat. When it's hot, add the parsnips and toss or stir them often, cooking for 5–6 minutes. You want to get them nice and golden on all sides but be careful as they do burn quickly.

Once the parsnips are golden, add the maple syrup and the rest of the seasoning. Toss well, making sure the parsnips are all coated, and cook for a further 3 minutes. The maple syrup will caramelize and crisp up the parsnips!

Serve straight away topped with thyme leaves.

Photograph on **page 105**.

Hasselback
POTATOES
WITH "CHEESE" SAUCE

Another beautiful potato dish! The beauty of the hasselback is that the flavour gets right into the potato and the slices crisp up beautifully.

500g (1lb 2oz) baby potatoes
3 tbsp rapeseed oil
1 tbsp dried rosemary
2 tsp sea salt
1 tsp cracked black pepper
zest of 1 lemon
1 garlic clove, crushed
handful of fresh chives,
 chopped, to serve
handful of dried cranberries,
 to serve

FOR THE "CHEESE" SAUCE
80g (½ cup) raw cashew nuts
120ml (scant ½ cup) filtered
 cold water
120ml (scant ½ cup) cold
 non-dairy milk
2 tbsp tapioca starch
3 tbsp nutritional yeast
1 tsp tahini
1 tsp white miso
pinch of sea salt and white pepper

Serves
6

Cooks In
50 minutes

Difficulty
5/10

GF

First up, preheat your oven to 180°C (350°F). Next, grab yourself a wooden spoon and sit a potato in the bowl of the spoon. Starting at one end, cut across the potato width-ways at 3mm (⅛in) intervals. The spoon will stop you cutting right through the potato. Carry on until you've sliced into all the potatoes, placing them into a roasting tray as you go.

Mix together the oil, rosemary, seasoning, lemon zest and garlic in a small mixing bowl, then use a pastry brush to brush the mixture all over the potatoes, making sure you get lots into the potato cuts. Once all the potatoes are coated, bake for 30–35 minutes, or until golden.

While the potatoes are in the oven, blitz together all the "cheese" sauce ingredients in a blender until smooth, then pour into a small saucepan.

Heat the sauce over a low heat, stirring constantly with a spatula, until it's thick and creamy.

When the potatoes are cooked, sprinkle over the chives and dried cranberries and serve them straight away with the sauce on the side or drizzled over the top.

Grilled
TENDERSTEM

This is my favourite way to serve tenderstem. Make sure you get lots of nice charred marks on the broccoli, the flavour is fire!

300g (10½oz) tenderstem broccoli
2 tbsp rapeseed oil
1 garlic clove, crushed
1 tbsp tamari soy sauce
pinch of cracked black pepper

Serves	Difficulty
4	**2/10**

Cooks In	**GF**
15 minutes	

Bring a large saucepan of water to the boil, then drop in the broccoli and cook for 3 minutes. Meanwhile preheat a griddle pan over a high heat.

After 3 minutes of cooking, remove the broccoli from the water with a slotted spoon and pat dry with kitchen paper.

Add the oil to the griddle pan followed by the garlic – spread it around the griddle pan with a wooden spoon. Immediately add the broccoli and cook for a couple of minutes and then turn over to cook the other side. Char lines are good – they will add great flavour.

Once nicely charred, turn off the heat and add the soy sauce and pepper to give a punch of umami flavour. Stir the broccoli a couple times, then serve.

Celeriac
PURÉE

This is luxurious, silky and creamy. It is great served with my
Rich mushroom and lentil parcels (page 86).

1 celeriac, peeled and chopped into
 small cubes
480ml (scant 2 cups) non-dairy milk
240ml (scant 1 cup) vegetable stock
juice of 1 lemon
½ tsp sea salt
½ tsp ground white pepper
2 tbsp extra virgin olive oil

Serves	Difficulty
4	**2/10**
Cooks In	**GF**
30 minutes	

Heat all the ingredients in a large saucepan over a medium heat, with the lid
on, for around 15 minutes. Stir every now and then. Once the celeriac is soft,
take the pan off the heat.

Let everything cool slightly before ladling it into a blender. Blitz until you have
a smooth purée. You may need to do this in batches if your blender is small.

Pour the purée back into the saucepan and check it for seasoning. If it's slightly
bland, add more salt, pepper and lemon juice to bring out the flavours.

Christmas CONDIMENTS

The essential condiments to spruce up your Christmas meal.

CRANBERRY AND ORANGE SAUCE
Makes 360g (13oz)

300g (3 cups) fresh cranberries
1 tsp grated fresh ginger
1 small cinnamon stick
1 Braeburn apple, grated
200g (1 cups) caster
 (superfine) sugar
240ml (1 cup) fresh orange juice

To sterilize your jars, place them in a large saucepan filled with cold water, place over a medium heat and bring to a simmer. Simmer for 3 minutes then turn off the heat. Carefully remove the jars from the water when you're ready to fill them.

Heat all the ingredients in a heavy-based saucepan over a low heat with the lid on. Cook for 15 minutes, stirring often.

Remove the jars from the hot water, spoon the sauce into the hot jars and seal. The sauce will keep for 4 weeks in the fridge.

HORSERADISH SAUCE
Makes enough for one meal

5cm (2in) fresh horseradish,
 grated and soaked in boiling
 water for 3 minutes
150g (¾ cup) vegan mayonnaise
zest and juice of ½ lemon
1 tbsp agave nectar
pinch of sea salt and pepper

Drain the soaked horseradish and mix with the other ingredients in a small bowl. Serve the same day as making.

MINT SAUCE
Makes 10 servings

30g (1oz) fresh mint leaves
4 tbsp white wine vinegar
5 tbsp boiling water
1 heaped tbsp caster
 (superfine) sugar
pinch of salt

Finely chop the mint leaves, then place in a heatproof jug. Add the rest of the ingredients, stir together and chill for at least 2 hours. Serve within 2–3 days.

Fluffy YORKSHIRE PUDDINGS

This was a hard recipe for me to crack, but after several attempts
I managed to veganize Yorkshire puddings! Make sure you get your baking
tin very hot for this!

260g (2 generous cups)
 self-raising flour
1½ tsp baking powder
1 tsp sea salt
480ml (2 cups) soy milk, or vegan
 milk of your choice
vegetable oil, for greasing

Makes
12

Cooks In
30 minutes

Difficulty
5/10

Preheat the oven to 210°C (420°F). Pour about 2 teaspoons of oil into each hole in a
12-hole Yorkshire-pudding baking tin.

Mix the flour, baking powder and salt together well in a large mixing bowl. Add the milk
to the bowl, whisk together until smooth, then pour the batter into a jug.

Now it's time to get the baking tray hot – place it into the oven for 4 minutes, then remove
the tray and quickly fill each hole with batter.

Carefully put the tray back into the oven for 16 minutes, or until the puddings are golden
brown and nicely risen.

Serve straight away.

Sweet Potato
AND CHESTNUT
STUFFING

Stuffing is one of my favourite parts of the Christmas dinner. I love this recipe, it has all the Christmassy flavours you could want. It tastes amazing when stuffed inside my "No-turkey" centre piece (page 64).

2 tbsp rapeseed oil
1 leek, finely chopped
2 garlic cloves, crushed
1 tbsp dried sage
2 tsp dried rosemary
½ tsp ground cinnamon
150g (5½oz) sweet potato, peeled, cubed and steamed
95g (½ cup) dried apricots, finely chopped

45g (¼ cup) dried cranberries, finely chopped
50g (¾ cup) breadcrumbs (gluten-free if necessary)
100g (3½oz) vacuum-packed chestnuts, chopped
200g (1 cup) canned chickpeas (garbanzos) or butterbeans
zest of 1 lemon

Serves
6

Cooks In
55 minutes

Difficulty
2/10

GF

First, preheat the oven to 180°C (350°F) and then line a medium-sized baking dish with greaseproof paper.

Heat the oil in a large, non-stick frying pan over a medium heat. Add the leek, garlic, herbs, cinnamon and cooked sweet potato and sauté until the leek has softened and the potato has browned. Add all the remaining ingredients and toss until well combined. Turn the heat off and, using an old-fashioned potato masher, lightly mash the mix. Break down any large chunks of sweet potato and the chickpeas/butterbeans.

Spoon the mixture into the lined baking dish and press it in to compact the mixture. Place the dish onto a baking tray and slide it into the oven to bake for 35–40 minutes. Once it's cooked, allow the stuffing to cool before taking it out of the dish and peeling off the paper.

> If you are using this to stuff the "turkey" roast (page 64), skip the final step.

Pan-Roasted
PUMPKIN WEDGES

——

Pumpkin is one of my favourite vegetables. Make sure you allow it to caramelize until golden-brown for maximum flavour.

1 small pumpkin or squash
3 tbsp rapeseed oil, plus a little extra
1 tbsp miso paste
pinch of sea salt and cracked black
  pepper
3 tbsp maple syrup
12 fresh sage leaves

TO SERVE
seeds from 1 pomegranate
pumpkin seeds

Serves
6

Cooks In
40 minutes

Difficulty
5/10

GF

Preheat your oven to 180°C (350°F). Using a serrated knife, top and tail the pumpkin. Cut it in half down the middle and scoop out the seeds. Wash the pulp off the seeds and roast in the oven for 12 minutes. Slice the pumpkin into 2.5-cm (1-in) thick wedges.

Bring a large saucepan of water to the boil, carefully add the pumpkin wedges and cook for 6–8 minutes. Drain the pumpkin into a colander, shake off any water, return to the empty saucepan and let them steam dry and cool slightly.

Whisk together the oil and miso paste in a large mixing bowl. Add the pumpkin wedges and give them a little toss to make sure they are nicely coated. Try not to break any.

Heat the oil in a large, non-stick frying pan over a medium heat and, when the pan is hot, fry a few wedges at a time (don't overcrowd the pan) for 3–4 minutes on each side, or until golden. Sprinkle over some salt and pepper and drizzle over a little of the syrup. Once golden on both sides, remove the wedges and transfer to a baking tray to keep warm in the oven. Repeat until you have fried all the wedges.

Leave the pan on the heat, add a couple tablespoons more of oil if there's none left in the pan. Throw in the sage leaves and cook for 2 minutes until crisp. Remove the sage leaves from the pan onto a couple of sheets of kitchen paper to soak up any excess oil. Serve the pumpkin wedges with the fried sage leaves, pomegranate seeds and the roasted pumpkin seeds sprinkled over the top.

Leftover
"TURKEY"
AND LEEK PIE

I don't think there's anything better than a warming pie the day after Christmas; it's the perfect way to use up any leftover veg from the big day.

2 tbsp rapeseed oil or water
2 leeks, washed and finely chopped
2 garlic cloves, crushed
160g (¾ cup) sweetcorn
200g (7oz) leftover "turkey" (page 64), stuffing removed and cut into cubes (or leftover vegetables)
1 tsp sea salt
2 tsp cracked black pepper
240ml (scant 1 cup) vegan-friendly white wine or vegetable stock

360ml (1½ cups) oat or soy cream or coconut milk
1 tbsp white miso paste
320g (11oz) ready-made vegan puff pastry
a little flour, for dusting

FOR THE GLAZE
4 tbsp maple syrup
4 tbsp non-dairy milk
4 tbsp vegetable oil

Serves
6

Cooks In
45 minutes

Difficulty
5/10

GFO
If gluten-free pastry is used

Heat the oil or water in a large saucepan placed over a medium heat. When hot, add the leeks and garlic and sauté for 3–4 minutes until soft. Add the sweetcorn and "turkey" (or veg), stir with a wooden spoon, and cook for a further 3 minutes. A little caramelization on the turkey will add a great flavour. Add the seasoning, then pour in the wine or stock, scraping any bits off the bottom to deglaze the pan. Cook for a further 3 minutes.

Stir in the cream and miso paste and simmer gently for 15 minutes – don't let it boil. After 15 minutes, it should be nice and creamy. Check the seasoning, and add more if needed. Scrape the filling into a 23cm (9in) pie dish and leave it to cool for around 25 minutes.

Meanwhile, preheat your oven to 180°C (350°F). Lightly flour a clean work surface and roll out your pastry to around 4mm (⅛in) thick and wide enough to fit over your pie dish. Carefully transfer the pastry and lay it over the filling, gently pressing around the edges of the pie dish to seal and trim off any overhanging pastry. Pinch the pastry around the edge of the pie dish to create a fluted edge. Get creative with the pastry trimmings – roll out again and cut into festive shapes or letters to decorate your pie, brushing with milk.

Mix the glaze ingredients together in a small bowl, then brush the glaze over the pie top and decoration. Bake on the lower shelf of the preheated oven for 30 minutes until the pastry is beautiful and golden. I like to brush over a little more glaze just before serving.

Christmas KORMA

I am so inspired by Indian food, especially dishes from Southern India. I dream of travelling to India one day, but for now, making delicious curries is enough. Make sure you cook the onions with the spices for the full 10 minutes to make sure they are golden and sweet. This is another amazing way of using up any leftover Christmas food.

5 tbsp vegetable oil
3 cardamom pods
2 cloves
2 fresh or frozen curry leaves
1 cinnamon stick
2 white onions, finely sliced
1 tsp sea salt
2 tsp caster (superfine) sugar
3 garlic cloves, peeled
thumb-sized piece of fresh
 ginger, peeled
½ tsp red chilli powder (add more
 if you like a kick)
½ tsp ground fenugreek
2 tsp ground cumin
1 tsp turmeric
2 tsp ground coriander
¼ tsp ground nutmeg
200g (7oz) leftover "turkey"
 (page 64) or "beef" (page 74),
 cut into chunks (optional)

2 sweet potatoes, peeled and cubed
400g (14oz) tin chickpeas
 (garbanzos), drained
25g (¼ cup) dried cranberries
3 tbsp coconut flour
400ml (14fl oz) tin full-fat
 coconut milk
240ml (scant 1 cup) vegetable stock

TO SERVE
2 tomatoes, cut into chunks
1 red onion, finely chopped
handful of fresh coriander (cilantro),
 finely chopped
juice of 1 lime
1 small green chilli, finely chopped
lime wedges
handful of dried cranberries

Serves
6

Cooks In
60 minutes

Difficulty
5/10

GFO
**If "turkey"and
"beef" are
left out**

CHRISTMAS KORMA RECIPE CONTINUED

Heat a large saucepan over a medium heat, add the oil followed by the cardamom pods, cloves, curry leaves and cinnamon stick. Cook for 2 minutes, then add the onions with the sea salt and sugar and stir constantly, cooking the onions for 8 minutes until golden and crisp but not burnt.

Put the garlic and ginger and a tablespoon of water into a blender and blitz until smooth. Add this paste to the crisp onions in the pan, cook for 1 minute, then add the spices. Cook for 4 minutes, stirring often.

Add the "meat", if using, the chickpeas and the cranberries. Continue to stir and cook for 4 more minutes.

Sprinkle in the coconut flour and stir well to mix it in, then add the coconut milk and stock. Give everything a good stir and turn the heat down low. Allow the curry to simmer away for 25 minutes, stirring every now and then, until the curry is thick and creamy.

To make a side salad, simply mix together the tomato, red onion, coriander (cilantro), lime and chilli. Serve alongside the curry with extra lime wedges and a sprinkling of cranberries.

GYROS

Who says the party has to stop after Christmas Day? These delicious kebabs are perfect party food. Use leftover "beef", cut into fine strips and seasoned up. Incredible!

FOR THE "MEAT"
200g (7oz) slow-roast "beef" (page 74), shredded
1 tsp smoked paprika
¼ tsp cayenne pepper
½ tsp ground cumin
½ tsp ground coriander
½ tsp dried garlic powder
2 tsp dried mixed herbs
pinch of sea salt and pepper
3 tbsp vegetable oil

FOR THE MINT YOGURT
285g (generous 1 cup) dairy-free plain yogurt
handful of fresh mint leaves, finely chopped
7.5cm (3in) piece of cucumber, deseeded and finely chopped

1 garlic clove, crushed
½ tsp paprika
1 tsp sea salt
juice of ½ lemon
2 tbsp extra virgin olive oil (optional)

FOR THE SALAD
2 baby gem lettuces, shredded
2 medium tomatoes
½ red onion, finely sliced
handful of fresh coriander (cilantro)
4–6 pickled chillis, from a jar

TO SERVE
toasted pitta bread or flat breads
hot sauce
lemon wedges

Serves
4

Cooks In
35 minutes

Difficulty
5/10

First up, mix all the ingredients for the "meat" together in a large mixing bowl. Cover and set aside to allow the flavours to mingle.

Meanwhile, put all the ingredients for the mint yogurt in a mixing bowl and stir well to combine. Cover with cling film (plastic wrap) and chill in the fridge until you're ready to serve.

Heat a large, non-stick pan over a high heat, then add the "meat" and cook for 4–5 minutes. Stir often and try and get lots of colour on the "meat".

To serve, fill your pitta breads or flat breads with generous amounts of the "meat", the various salad elements and a dollop of mint yogurt. A drizzle of hot sauce adds a nice kick and a squeeze of lemon juice brings all the flavours together.

Bubble & Squeak
PATTIES

You can use whatever leftovers you have for bubble and squeak. This is a basic guide to using up some of the dishes from the previous chapters. My tip for the perfect bubble and squeak is to make sure you have plenty of potatoes – these will help bind all the leftovers together – so when you cook roasties, make more than you need so you have enough left over!

5–6 leftover Roasties (page 102)
2–3 leftover Orange-glazed carrots (page 104)
handful of Braised red cabbage (page 98)
8–10 Sexy sprouts (page 100)
4–5 Sticky beetroot (page 97)
3–4 Maple pan-roasted parsnips (page 106)
4–5 stems of Grilled tenderstem broccoli (page 110)
handful of fresh parsley, stems included

handful of chopped "meat" (leftovers from any of the "meat" recipes)
4–5 tbsp plain (all-purpose) flour, plus extra for dusting
zest of 1 lemon
2 tbsp Cranberry and orange sauce (page 112)
4 tbsp Rich white wine gravy (page 67)
3–4 tbsp rapeseed oil, for frying

TO SERVE
1 avocado
mixed leaf salad

Serves
4

Cooks In
40 minutes

Difficulty
5/10

GFO
If seitan is left out – nut roast is a nice addition

Preheat the oven to 180°C (350°F) and line a baking tray with greaseproof paper. First up, mash up the roasties in a mixing bowl using an old-fashioned potato masher.

Put the other vegetables and the parsley into a blender and pulse until the vegetables are all a similar size. Add these to the bowl of potato, followed by the chopped "meat" then mix everything together thoroughly. Stir in the flour, lemon zest, cranberry sauce and gravy.

Lightly flour your hands and the lined baking tray. Divide the mixture into four and use your hands to form into individual patties, approximately burger-sized.

Heat the oil in a non-stick frying pan over a medium heat and add a couple of patties. Cook for 3–4 minutes on each side until golden, then carefully remove them from the pan and place them into the lined baking tray. Continue with the remaining patties. Pop the tray into the preheated oven and bake the patties for 12 minutes. Serve straight away, simply with avocado and salad leaves.

Sweet Chilli,
CRISPY "BEEF"
STIR FRY

Another great way to use up leftover "beef", playing on Asian flavours.
The beef strips get super crispy when fried. Use any combination of
leftover vegetables that you fancy.

FOR THE SWEET CHILLI SAUCE
250ml (1 cup) filtered water
125ml (½ cup) white wine vinegar
125 ml (½ cup) tomato purée (paste)
2 tbsp Sriracha
1 tbsp sweet chilli flakes (or hot,
 if you prefer)
3 tbsp caster (superfine) sugar

FOR THE CRISPY "BEEF"
200g (7oz) leftover "beef", cut into
 thin strips (page 74)
125g (1 cup) cornflour (cornstarch)
1 tsp sea salt
250ml (1 cup) ice-cold
 sparkling water
500ml (2 cups) vegetable oil,
 for frying

FOR THE STIR-FRY VEG
4 leftover Orange-glazed carrots
 (page 104), evenly chopped
4–5 leftover Grilled tenderstem
 (page 110), evenly chopped
1 red onion, finely sliced
2 baby pak choi, quartered
2 tbsp sesame oil

TO SERVE
rice or noodles
toasted sesame seeds
handful fresh coriander
 (cilantro) leaves

Serves
4

Cooks In
45 minutes

Difficulty
5/10

GFO
**If "beef" is
left out —use
mushrooms
instead**

First up, prepare the sweet chilli sauce – add everything to a small saucepan and
whisk until combined. Place over a very low heat and let the sauce simmer away
for 15 minutes to gradually thicken up. Stir from time to time.

Heat the vegetable oil in a wok or large saucepan, making sure the oil doesn't come
up higher than half way. Alternatively, use a deep-fat fryer set at 180°C (350°F).

Mix the cornflour, salt and sparkling water together in a bowl to form the batter.

SWEET CHILLI, CRISPY "BEEF" STIR FRY RECIPE CONTINUED

Test if the oil is hot enough to fry the crispy beef – place a cube of bread into the oil and if it bubbles and floats to the surface, your oil is ready.

Coat a few strips of "beef" in the batter, and make sure they are well covered. Lower the coated strips carefully into the oil a few at a time. Try not to drop them together in one clump as they will stick together. Fry the strips for 3–4 minutes until crisp. Once golden, lift out of the oil with a slotted spoon onto a plate lined with kitchen paper to absorb any excess oil. Fry the rest of the "beef", then set aside while you quickly stir fry the vegetables.

Heat a large, non-stick frying pan over a high heat. Add the sesame oil, followed by the vegetables and stir fry for 3–4 minutes. If you're using fresh vegetables, you may need to cook them for slightly longer. When the vegetables have lightly browned, add the crispy "beef" strips followed by a couple of ladles of sweet chilli sauce. Toss the pan to make sure everything is coated in the sauce and serve immediately with rice or noodles, toasted sesame seeds and fresh coriander.

ZESTY WARM SALAD

—

Something a little lighter, after maybe over-indulging on Christmas Day!
This salad is a great zesty pick-me-up.

200g (7oz) cavolo nero or curly kale, stems removed, roughly chopped
180g (1 cup) wild rice, cooked and chilled
180g (1 cup) quinoa, cooked and chilled
4 tbsp mixed seeds (pumpkin, sesame, linseed, sunflower)
75g (½ cup) walnuts, crushed
50g (½ cup) dried cranberries, chopped
juice of 2 lemons

handful of fresh basil leaves, chopped
5 tbsp extra virgin olive oil
3 tbsp balsamic vinegar
1 tsp sea salt
1 tsp cracked black pepper
5–6 Pan-roasted pumpkin wedges, cubed (page 117), optional

TO SERVE
2 blood oranges, peeled and segmented

Serves
4

Cooks In
25 minutes

Difficulty
2/10

GF

Bring a large saucepan of water to the boil, add the cavolo nero or kale and blanch for 2 minutes before draining into a colander. Let the leaves cool slightly.

Put the rest of the salad ingredients into a large mixing bowl and stir well to combine everything. Once the leaves have cooled, fold them through the rest of the salad.

Serve the salad straight away with the orange segments.

TIRAMISU

I was so pleased when I veganized this Italian classic. It's the perfect festive dessert and even more showstopping when you serve it with a sparkler!

FOR THE SPONGE
250ml (1 cup) almond milk
1 tbsp apple cider vinegar
1 tsp vanilla bean paste
50g (¼ cup) vegan spread
215g (1¾ cups) self-raising flour
 (or gluten-free flour)
230g (generous 1 cup) unrefined
 caster (superfine) sugar
pinch sea salt

FOR THE CREAM
2 x 400g (14oz) tins coconut cream
170g (6oz) vegan cream cheese
1 tbsp cacao powder
3 tbsp icing (confectioner's) sugar
120ml (½ cup) good-quality coffee,
 brewed over ice
4 tbsp rum, or to taste

TOPPINGS
grated dark chocolate
coffee beans

Serves
6

Cooks In
60 minutes

Difficulty
5/10

GF
**If gluten-free
flour is used**

Preheat your oven to 180°C (350°F) and line a 5cm (2in) deep 20 x 30cm (8 x 12in) baking tray with non-stick baking paper.

First up, the sponge! Put the almond milk, apple cider vinegar, vanilla paste and vegan spread into a small saucepan over a low heat. Measure the flour, sugar and salt into a large mixing bowl. When the spread has melted, pour the milk mixture into the dry ingredients and fold together. Scrape the batter into your lined baking tray and level out.

Place the tray into the oven to bake for 12–15 minutes, or until golden and springy to the touch, then turn out the sponge onto a wire rack to cool completely.

Whisk the coconut cream, cream cheese, cacao powder and icing sugar together in a large mixing bowl until fully incorporated. Add a few tablespoons of coffee and rum, then taste. Adjust the flavours according to how you like it.

Cut 12 discs of sponge to fit into your serving glasses. Pop a sponge disc in the base of each glass, then a spoonful of cream, then another sponge disc. Drizzle in a little more coffee and spoon in another layer of cream. Top each tiramisu with chocolate shavings and a couple coffee beans. Eat straight away or chill in the fridge for up to one day.

Christmas
PUDDING

The ultimate vegan Christmas pudding – boozy, fruity and moreish!

100g (¾ cup) sultanas
100g (generous ½ cup) dried mixed peel
100g (generous ½ cup) chopped dates
50g (¼ cup) dried cherries
25g (1 oz) crystallized ginger, chopped
120ml (½ cup) rum or brandy
juice of 1 orange
zest and juice of 1 lemon
1 bay leaf
1 tsp ground nutmeg

1 tsp ground mixed spice
1 tsp ground cinnamon
½ tsp sea salt
75g (⅓ cup) demerara or coconut sugar
2 tbsp black treacle (molasses)
1 Braeburn apple, grated
115g (scant ½ cup) vegan spread, plus extra for greasing
45g (½ cup) breadcrumbs
95g (¾ cup) plain (all-purpose) flour
½ tsp baking powder

Serves
6

Cooks In
7 hours

Difficulty
7/10

The day before, put the dried fruit plus the alcohol, orange and lemon juice and the bay leaf into a large bowl. Stir well to mix, cover and leave for at least 12 hours to plump up.

The next day, grease a 1 litre (2 pint) pudding bowl with vegan spread, then line the base with a circle of greaseproof paper to ensure the pudding comes out once cooked.

Remove the bay leaf from the fruit. Add the lemon zest, spices, salt, sugar, treacle and apple and mix. Stir in the vegan spread and breadcrumbs. Sift in the flour and baking powder and fold in. Spoon the mixture into the pudding bowl, leaving a 2.5cm (1in) gap at the top. Cover with greaseproof paper, then a sheet of foil and tie with cook's string.

Put an upturned ramekin in the bottom of a saucepan. Sit the pudding on top, then pour in boiling water half way up the sides of the pudding. Cover and simmer over a low heat for 5 hours, topping up the water when needed. Lift the pudding out and leave to cool.

Store for up to a month before serving. Steam again in the same way for 30 minutes. Add 2 shots of vegan-friendly brandy to a saucepan and heat over a low heat for 2 minutes. Light the brandy with a match, then carefully pour over the pudding for that festive flame.

Cinnamon-spiced
APPLE
CRUMBLE

This is a great dessert option if you're looking for something slightly healthier. It's gluten free and refined sugar free but still divine.

5 crisp eating apples (such
 as Braeburn)
100g (scant ½ cup) coconut sugar
2 tbsp coconut oil
1 tsp vanilla bean paste or
 1 vanilla pod
2 tsp ground cinnamon

FOR THE TOPPING
75g (scant ½ cup) rice flour

75g (¾ cup) almond flour
 (or coconut flour if nut-free)
pinch of sea salt
115g (½ cup) vegan spread
100g (scant ½ cup) coconut sugar
45g (½ cup) gluten-free
 porridge oats

TO SERVE
vegan ice cream or custard
a few spigs of fresh mint

Serves
4

Cooks In
40 minutes

Difficulty
2/10

GF

Preheat your oven to 180°C (350°F). Core the apples, then cut three of them into 1cm (⅓in) cubes and grate the other two. Leave the skin on as that's where the best flavour is!

Put the coconut sugar into a large saucepan placed over a medium heat and wait for the sugar to melt down. Keep an eye on it to make sure it doesn't burn; it should only take 2 minutes. Add the coconut oil followed by the grated apple and cook for a couple of minutes for the apple to almost melt down.

Stir in the vanilla pod and seeds and cinnamon and cook for 1 more minute while stirring, then add the cubed apple. Turn the heat down to its lowest setting, pop the lid on and cook for 15 minutes, stirring every now and then. Remove the vanilla pod.

Meanwhile prepare your topping. Put the flour, ground almonds and sea salt into a large mixing bowl and stir to combine. Add the spread and use your fingers to rub together until it starts to become like breadcrumbs. Stir in the sugar and the oats.

Once the apples have softened, pour the filling into an 8cm (3in) deep 23cm (9in) baking dish. Cover with the crumble topping, then bake in the oven for 15 minutes, or until the crumble is golden. Serve with vegan ice cream or custard, garnished with a sprig of mint.

Crème
BRÛLÉE
TARTLETS

Another classic dish that I was so pleased to veganize. Turning it into a tart was a total winner! The filling is so creamy, perfect with the crisp pastry.

FOR THE PASTRY
250g (2 cups) plain
  (all-purpose) flour
125g (1 cup) icing
  (confectioner's) sugar
pinch of salt
pinch of ground cinnamon
125g (½ cup) vegan spread
about 2 tbsp almond milk

FOR THE GLAZE
3 tbsp maple syrup
2 tbsp vegetable oil

FOR THE CRÈME BRÛLÉE FILLING
400ml (14fl oz) tin of coconut milk
1 vanilla pod, seeds scraped out
300ml (1¼ cup) almond milk
4 tbsp of cornflour (cornstarch)
4 tbsp icing (confectioner's) sugar

6 tbsp caster (superfine) sugar,
  to finish

Makes
6 tartlets

Cooks In
60 minutes

Difficulty
7/10

GFO
If pastry is left out – make brûlées in ramekins

Combine the flour, sugar, salt and cinnamon together in a mixing bowl. Add the vegan spread and rub into the dry ingredients with your fingers until the mix is a breadcrumb-like consistency.

Pour in enough milk to bring the mixture together to form a ball of dough and pick up all the bits from the bowl. Give it a slight knead for 2 minutes, then wrap the dough in cling film (plastic wrap) and pop it into the freezer to chill for 25 minutes.

Preheat your oven to 180°C (350°F) and grease 6 loose-bottomed 10cm (4in) tartlet tins. Remove your pastry from the freezer and roll it out to about 3mm (⅛in) onto a sheet of greaseproof paper (which makes it easier when lifting in to the tart tins). Line the tins with the pastry, gently pressing into the corners and fluted edges, and trim off any excess over-hanging. Cut 6 circles of greaseproof paper to sit over the pastry cases and fill with baking beans.

Put the tins onto a baking sheet, transfer to the oven to blind bake the pastry for 6 minutes, then remove the beans and paper and cook for a further 6 minutes, or until golden.

Spiced
HOT CHOCOLATE

The best hot chocolate ever!

1l (4 cups) non-dairy milk
4 tbsp cacao powder
1 tsp vanilla bean paste
¼ tsp ground ginger
¼ tsp ground cinnamon
4 tbsp maple syrup
100g (3½oz) dairy-free
 chocolate, grated

TO SERVE
2 tsp cacao powder
vegan marshmallows (optional)

Serves
4

Cooks In
25 minutes

Difficulty
2/10

GF

Heat all the ingredients for the hot chocolate (except the grated chocolate) together in a saucepan until it reaches a light simmer, then add the chocolate. Whisk until the chocolate has melted – don't let it boil.

Serve your hot chocolate in mugs , topped with a sprinkle of cacao powder and vegan marshmallows, if you like.

Grilled Mango
& COCONUT PANNA COTTA

A more tropical inspired Christmas dessert because, of course, not all countries are cold at Christmas! I recommend using 5cm (2½in) stainless steel dariole moulds or plastic mini jelly moulds.

400ml (14fl oz) tin of full-fat coconut milk
1 vanilla pod, seeds scraped out (or 2 tsp vanilla bean paste)
1 shot vegan-friendly rum, optional
250ml (1 cup) non-dairy milk
65g (½ cup) cornflour (cornstarch)
5 tbsp coconut honey or maple syrup

FOR THE MANGO DRESSING
200g (7oz) mango, peeled and cubed

120ml (½ cup) water
½ tsp dried chilli flakes

FOR THE GRILLED MANGO
1 tbsp coconut oil, plus extra for greasing
½ mango, peeled and cut into 2.5cm (1in) thick slices
2 tbsp coconut sugar

TO SERVE
fresh mint leaves, chopped coconut flakes, lightly toasted

Makes
6

Cooks In
60 minutes

Difficulty
5/10

GF

Lightly grease 6 moulds with coconut oil and place on a baking tray. Heat the coconut milk and rum in a saucepan over a low heat. Add the vanilla pod and seeds. Allow to infuse while you whisk the non-dairy milk, cornflour and coconut honey together in a bowl until smooth. Scrape the cornflour mixture into the saucepan and stir until it has thickened up, about 4–5 minutes.

Remove from the heat, remove the vanilla pod and spoon the mix into your moulds. Tap them on the surface to level out. Cover with cling film (plastic wrap) and refrigerate for at least 3 hours.

Blitz all the dressing ingredients in a blender until smooth. If the dressing is too thick, add more water. Before serving, heat a griddle pan over a high heat. Melt the coconut oil, then add the mango slices and griddle until lightly charred, then sprinkle over coconut sugar for additional caramelization. Griddle the mango on all sides for around 3–4 minutes.

To turn the panna cotta out of their moulds, simply dip the base of each mould into hot water to loosen them, then invert onto a serving plate. Serve with plenty of dressing, grilled mango and coconut flakes.

Chocolate Orange Raw
"CHEESECAKE"

Another showstopper... a creamy "cheesecake". This is sweetened with natural sugar and totally raw. Chocolate orange – the taste of Christmas.

FOR THE BASE
170g (1⅔ cups) ground almonds
80g (½ cup) macadamia nuts
40g (½ cup) pecans
3 tbsp agave nectar
3 tbsp coconut oil
1 tbsp peanut butter
pinch of sea salt

FOR THE FILLING
340g (2½ cups) raw cashew nuts,
 soaked for at least 1 hour
240ml (1 cup) coconut oil, melted
240ml (1 cup) almond milk

400ml (14fl oz) tin coconut milk
8 tbsp maple syrup or agave nectar
2 tsp vanilla extract
juice and zest of 1 orange
2 tbsp organic cacao powder

FOR THE CHOCOLATE DRIZZLE
5 tbsp coconut oil, melted
4 tbsp organic cacao powder
2 tbsp agave nectar

TOPPING SUGGESTIONS
fresh or dried orange slices, physalis, pecans, fresh mint leaves

Serves
6–8

Made In
45 minutes + setting time

Difficulty
5/10

GF

Line a 23cm (9in) loose-bottomed cake tin with greaseproof paper. Add all the base ingredients to a blender and blitz until smooth. Spoon into the tin to form a 1cm (½in) base, pressing into the tin until compact. Freeze. Alternatively, use small individual moulds.

Put half of the filling ingredients in your blender and add the 2 tbsp cacao powder and blitz until super-smooth to make the chocolate layer. Pour this into your chilled tin, on top of the base, and return to the freezer for at least 45 minutes to set.

Wash out your blender, then add the remaining half of the filling ingredients together with the orange juice and zest to make the orange layer. Blitz until smooth. Remove the tin from the freezer and pour over the orange filling. Make sure it is smooth and level and place the "cheesecake" carefully back into the freezer to set fully for at least 3 hours.

Remove the "cheesecake" from the freezer 20 minutes before serving. Pour boiling water over a tea-towel, wait until you can handle it, then lay it around the cake tin for a few seconds to melt the edges – you can then release the "cheesecake" from the tin easily.

Mix together the drizzle ingredients in a bowl with a fork until smooth. Drizzle around the edge of the "cheesecake", then decorate with orange, physalis, pecans and mint.

Fried Doughnut PROFITEROLES

I came up with this recipe while wracking my brains trying to veganize choux pastry. I thought, why not combine two big desserts, doughnuts and profiteroles? The outcome is unbelievable!

FOR THE DOUGHNUT PROFITEROLES
120ml (½ cup) almond milk
5 tbsp vegan spread
250g (2 cups) plain (all-purpose)
 flour, plus extra for dusting
2 tsp baking powder
pinch of sea salt
50g (scant ½ cup) icing
 (confectioner's) sugar
1.5 l (6⅓ cups) vegetable oil,
 for frying

FOR THE CREAM FILLING
320ml (1⅓ cups) coconut cream
1 shot Baileys Almande or vegan
 liqueur (optional)
1 tsp vanilla bean paste
2 tbsp icing (confectioner's) sugar

FOR THE CHOCOLATE SAUCE
300ml (1¼ cups) almond milk
3 tbsp agave nectar
100g (3½oz) dairy-free dark
 chocolate, finely chopped

FOR THE SUGAR STRING
200g (1 cup) caster (superfine) sugar

Serves
4–6

Cooks In
60 minutes

Difficulty
7/10

First up, make the doughnut profiteroles. Put the milk and spread in a small saucepan over a low heat to melt and mix together.

Combine all the dry ingredients in a mixing bowl, then pour in the melted spread and milk and mix with a spatula until it forms a wet dough. Lightly flour your hands and your work surface. Pick up around 2 tablespoons of dough at a time and roll it in your hands to form neat balls.

Line a baking tray with kitchen paper and preheat a deep-fat fryer to 170°C (340°F) or half fill a large saucepan with the vegetable oil and set over a medium heat. Test if it's hot enough by dropping in a little piece of dough – if it bubbles and floats to the surface, the oil is ready.

FRIED DOUGHNUT PROFITEROLES RECIPE CONTINUED

Fry 3 to 4 balls at a time for 3–4 minutes, or until golden brown. You may need to flip them over half way through cooking. When cooked, lift them out of the oil using a spider or slotted spoon, gently shaking off excess oil, and transfer the profiteroles straight onto the lined tray and set aside to cool.

To make the whipped cream, put all the ingredients in a mixing bowl and whisk together until thick and creamy. Set aside until you're ready to serve.

To make the chocolate sauce, pour the milk and agave nectar into a saucepan and place over a low heat to warm gradually. Meanwhile, tip the chopped chocolate into a mixing bowl. When the milk is piping hot, pour it over the chocolate and stir until smooth and all the chocolate has melted.

Cut the profiteroles in half lengthways. Pipe or spoon generous amounts of the cream onto the bottom halves and stick the tops back on.

Before serving, melt the caster (superfine) sugar in a heavy-based pan until golden.

Stack your profiteroles on a serving plate then drizzle over the chocolate sauce. Finally, using a spoon, spin the melted sugar around the stack. Be extremely careful as the sugar will be super hot.

A MORNING-AFTER PICK-ME-UP

If you need a helping hand after an indulgent Christmas day, this is the perfect drink for you.

2 cucumbers
2 celery sticks
2 wedges of watermelon
2 handfuls of kale
2 handfuls of spinach
thumb-sized piece of fresh ginger
1 kiwi
1 apple

Serves
2–4

Cut the watermelon down into pieces so it will fit into your juicer. Add all the ingredients to the juicer and juice.

Serve with ice and enjoy a blast of energy after drinking!

"Cheese" & Pâté
BOARD

It wouldn't be Christmas without the cheeseboard and why can't us vegans have one too? These are indulgent "cheeses" that will really impress.

TRUFFLE CREAM "CHEESE"
Makes 10 servings

150g (1 cup) raw cashew nuts
120ml (½ cup) cashew nut milk
2 tbsp nutritional yeast flakes
1 tbsp fresh lemon juice
pinch of sea salt and white pepper
2 tbsp truffle oil, or to taste

First up, you want to quick-soak the cashews (see tip). Drain the water from the nuts, put them into a blender with all the other ingredients and blitz for 15 seconds. Stir with a spatula, then blend again until smooth.

The smoother the better, so add a little more milk if it needs it. Once smooth, place it into a sealed container for up to 3 days or until you're ready to serve.

> To quick-soak nuts, pop them into a heatproof container and cover with boiling water. Leave for 15 minutes to soften.
>
> SUGGESTED ACCOMPANIMENTS
> Vegan crackers, toasted bread, olives, mixed nuts, fresh vegetables (such as carrot sticks and celery), grapes and fresh figs.

PISTACHIO AND CRANBERRY "CHEESE" LOG
Makes 2 logs

150g (1 cup) raw cashew nuts
150g (1 cup) macadamia nuts
1 tsp dried garlic
120ml (½ cup) filtered water
120ml (½ cup) cashew nut milk
zest and juice of 1 lemon
3 tbsp nutritional yeast
1 tsp white miso paste
1 tsp sea salt
5 tbsp chopped pistachios
3 tbsp chopped dried cranberries

Quick-soak the nuts (see tip). Drain off the water and tip the nuts into the blender with the rest of the ingredients. Blitz until smooth – you may need to scrape the sides a couple of times. If needed, add a touch more water. Lay a sheet of muslin (cheesecloth) inside a sieve set over a bowl. Spoon the "cheese" mixture into the muslin and tie the corners together. Twist the muslin a little to squeeze the "cheese" and start draining the water. Transfer to the fridge for at least 24 hours to let all the water drip out.

Lay a piece of cling film (plastic wrap) on your worksurface, then scatter with the pistachios and cranberries. Spoon half of the drained "cheese" into the centre of the cling film. Roll up, then twist each end tightly. Repeat with the second log. Place in the freezer for 2 hours to set before serving.

"CHEESE" & PÂTÉ BOARD RECIPE CONTINUED

LEMON AND DILL "CHEESE"
Makes 6–8 servings

a little coconut oil, for greasing
90g (¾ cup) cashews
180ml (¾ cup) boiled water
240ml (scant 1 cup) soy milk
2 tbsp tapioca starch
2 tbsp nutritional yeast
zest of ½ a lemon, plus extra for serving
2 tsp dried dill, plus extra for serving
1 tbsp lemon juice
2 tbsp agar agar powder
pinch of sea salt and white pepper

Grease two 9cm (3½in) moulds or containers with a little coconut oil – I like little round "cheeses" so I use small cake tins or ramekins.

Quick-soak the nuts (see tip on page 156). Once the nuts have softened, drain and tip them into a blender with all the other ingredients. Blend until you have a super-smooth, creamy mixture.

Scrape the mixture into a saucepan. Using a spatula, stir the mixture over a low heat until it starts to thicken. Continue to stir until the mixture is really thick and has a melted cheese-like consistency.

It's essential that you stir continuously as it can easily catch on the bottom, which totally spoils the flavour, so try not to have any distractions.

Remove the pan from the heat, pour the "cheese" into your prepared containers and chill in the fridge for 2 hours, or until set through. This "cheese" will keep for 4–5 days in the fridge.

To serve, remove the "cheese" from the container, sprinkle over some additional dried dill and lemon zest, slice and enjoy!

MUSHROOM PÂTÉ
Makes 6–8 servings

360ml (1½ cup) vegan-friendly
 white wine
30g (1oz) dried mushrooms
 (such as porcini, shiitake)
3 tbsp coconut oil
2 banana shallots, finely sliced
3 garlic cloves, crushed
2 tbsp fresh thyme leaves
3 portobello mushrooms, diced
500g (1lb 2oz) chestnut mushrooms,
 brushed clean and diced
1 tsp miso paste
½ tsp smoked (or regular) sea salt
1 tsp cracked black pepper
120ml (½ cup) soy or oat cream

Heat the wine gently in a saucepan until just simmering. Put the dried mushrooms in a heatproof bowl, pour over the wine, and let the mushrooms rehydrate for 10 minutes.

Melt the coconut oil in a large, non-stick saucepan over a medium heat. Add the shallot, garlic and thyme. Sauté for 3–4 minutes, stirring, until softened and lightly browned. Add the fresh mushrooms and cook, stirring often, for 5 minutes (they will shrink dramatically as they cook). Cover with a lid in between stirring.

Scoop the mushrooms out of the wine and add them to the pan. Pour the wine through a fine sieve into the saucepan to get rid of any grit left behind. Use a wooden spoon to scrape any bits off the bottom of the pan – you want all that flavour. Add the miso paste and seasoning, stir, then let the mushrooms cook for 10 minutes over a low heat, uncovered, so the liquids evaporate.

Remove from the heat, leave to cool to room temperature, then tip into a blender with the cream. Blitz until smooth. Keep in sterilized jars (page 112) in the fridge for up to 5 days.

Christmas
COOKIES

——

Light, crunchy cookies... perfect to give away as gifts.

125g (½ cup) vegan spread
60g (½ cup) icing (confectioner's)
 sugar, plus extra for dusting
60g (⅓ cup) light brown sugar
1 tsp vanilla bean paste
275g (generous 2 cups) plain
 (all-purpose) flour, plus extra
 for dusting
½ tsp baking powder
½ tsp bicarbonate of soda

Makes
12–14

Cooks In
45 minutes

Difficulty
5/10

GF
**If gluten-free
flour is used**

Beat together the spread, both sugars and vanilla paste with a wooden spoon in a large mixing bowl until creamy. Sift in the flour and raising agents and bring together until it forms a ball of dough. Lightly knead the dough for a couple of minutes, then wrap it in cling film (plastic wrap) and chill in the fridge for at least an hour.

Preheat the oven to 170°C (340°F) and line a large baking tray with greaseproof paper.

Lightly flour your work surface and rolling pin and roll out the dough to around 4mm (⅙in) thick. Use festive cookie cutters to cut the dough, placing the raw cookies onto the lined baking tray as you go. Bake for 12–15 minutes or until lightly golden. Remove from the oven and let the cookies cool slightly on the tray before carefully transferring them to a wire rack to cool completely.

When the cookies are cool, dust with icing (confectioner's) sugar.

Photograph on **page 165**.

Christmas
COOKIES

Light, crunchy cookies... perfect to give away as gifts.

125g (½ cup) vegan spread
60g (½ cup) icing (confectioner's)
 sugar, plus extra for dusting
60g (⅓ cup) light brown sugar
1 tsp vanilla bean paste
275g (generous 2 cups) plain
 (all-purpose) flour, plus extra
 for dusting
½ tsp baking powder
½ tsp bicarbonate of soda

Makes
12–14

Cooks In
45 minutes

Difficulty
5/10

GF
**If gluten-free
flour is used**

Beat together the spread, both sugars and vanilla paste with a wooden spoon in a large mixing bowl until creamy. Sift in the flour and raising agents and bring together until it forms a ball of dough. Lightly knead the dough for a couple of minutes, then wrap it in cling film (plastic wrap) and chill in the fridge for at least an hour.

Preheat the oven to 170°C (340°F) and line a large baking tray with greaseproof paper.

Lightly flour your work surface and rolling pin and roll out the dough to around 4mm (⅛in) thick. Use festive cookie cutters to cut the dough, placing the raw cookies onto the lined baking tray as you go. Bake for 12–15 minutes or until lightly golden. Remove from the oven and let the cookies cool slightly on the tray before carefully transferring them to a wire rack to cool completely.

When the cookies are cool, dust with icing (confectioner's) sugar.

Photograph on **page 165**.

EDIBLE

gifts

Healthy Chocolate
ROCKY ROAD

Chocolatey goodness, these are filled with nuts and dried fruit.
Another amazing stocking filler.

220g (1 cup) raw cacao butter,
  chopped
125g (1 cup) raw cacao powder
175g (½ cup) maple syrup or
  agave nectar
1 tsp vanilla bean paste

or use 2 x 100g (3½oz) bars
  dairy-free dark chocolate

FOR THE TOPPINGS
160g (1 cup) chopped dried fruit
  (pineapple, apricot, banana,
  cranberries, mango)
150g (1 cup) mixed nuts
40g (½ cup) coconut flakes

Serves
12

Cooks In
30 minutes

Difficulty
2/10

GF

Line a baking tray with greaseproof paper.

Melt the chopped cacao butter in a heatproof mixing bowl set over a small saucepan of simmering water, then lift the bowl off the saucepan.

Whisk in the cacao powder until fully incorporated. Stir in the syrup and vanilla bean paste. Give it a quick taste to see if it's sweet enough (add a little more syrup if not), then quickly pour the chocolate onto your lined baking tray.

Alternatively, melt the two bars of dairy-free dark chocolate.

Before it sets, sprinkle over the chopped fruit, nuts and coconut flakes.

Transfer the rocky road to the fridge to set for at least 3 hours. Break into shards before wrapping in paper and giving it to your loved ones. Don't forget to tell them to keep it in the fridge.

Photograph on **page 165**.

Coconut
BOUNTIES

I love chocolate-covered coconut bars and they are so simple to veganize.
They are light, refreshing and another perfect edible gift idea!

FOR THE FILLING
180g (2 cups) desiccated coconut
160ml (5½ fl oz) coconut cream
125g (½ cup) coconut oil
4 tbsp coconut honey or maple syrup
1 tsp vanilla bean paste

FOR THE COATING
2 x 100g (3½ oz) bars dairy-free
 chocolate, chopped

Makes
8 large bars

Makes In
**30 minutes +
setting time**

Difficulty
5/10

GF

Line a 23cm (9in) square, loose-bottom cake tin with greaseproof paper.

Put all the filling ingredients in your blender and whizz until all the ingredients are well incorporated. Tip the mixture into the lined cake tin and push it into the corners. Press the mixture down with the back of a wooden spoon until it's level, then pop the cake tin into your freezer to set while you melt the chocolate.

Melt the chopped chocolate in a heatproof mixing bowl set over a small saucepan of simmering water. When all the chocolate has melted, lift the bowl off the pan and set aside to cool slightly.

Take the chilled filling out of the freezer and slice the coconut into eight bars. Warm your knife under hot water before slicing each time to make this easier.

Line a baking sheet with greaseproof paper. Use a fork to dip the coconut pieces individually in the chocolate, shake off any excess chocolate and place them on the lined tray. Once you've coated all the pieces, pop them in the fridge to set for 2 hours.

Jaffa CAKES

Vegan jaffa cakes – who would have thought it! The wonders of agar agar.
These are very simple to make. Give any vegan these wrapped up in a box
and you will make their Christmas.

FOR THE SPONGE LAYER
coconut oil, for greasing
120ml (½ cup) soy milk
55g (¼ cup) vegan spread
1 tsp orange essence
120g (1 cup) plain (all-purpose) flour
100g (½ cup) unrefined caster
 (superfine) sugar
1 tsp baking powder
¼ tsp fine sea salt
¼ tsp ground cinnamon
¼ tsp ground nutmeg

FOR THE ORANGE JELLY
2 tbsp agar agar flakes
120ml (½ cup) cold water
240ml (1 cup) freshly squeezed
 orange juice
2 tbsp caster (superfine) sugar

FOR THE CHOCOLATE TOPPING
2 x 100g (3½oz) bars dairy-free
 chocolate, finely chopped
pinch of sea salt

Makes
24

Cooks In
60 minutes

Difficulty
7/10

GF
**If gluten-free
flour is used**

Make the jelly first as it needs 2 hours to set. Line a baking tray with cling film (plastic wrap). Heat the agar agar and water in a saucepan over a medium heat. Bring to the boil, whisk until the flakes disappear, remove from the heat and add the orange juice and sugar. Whisk until combined, pour onto your lined baking tray and place in the fridge until set. Preheat the oven to 180°C (360°F). Grease two non-stick muffin trays with coconut oil.

Put the soy milk, vegan spread and orange essence into a saucepan and set over a low heat until the spread has melted and everything has mixed together. Combine the flour, sugar, baking powder, salt and spices in a mixing bowl. Make a well in the middle and pour in the orange-milk mixture. Stir well until you have a thick batter. Spoon a couple tablespoons of the batter into each hole in your greased tray. Smooth the mixture level, then bake for 8 minutes until lightly golden. Allow to cool slightly in the trays before transferring to a wire rack to cool completely.

Put the chocolate into a heatproof bowl set over a saucepan of simmering water. When melted, lift the bowl off the pan, allow the chocolate to cool slightly, then stir in the salt. Remove the set jelly from the fridge and use a round cutter (just smaller than the cake bases) to cut the jelly. Lift the rounds onto the top of each cake base, then spoon over the chocolate. Spread the coated jaffa cakes out on a plate and allow to set completely in the fridge. It should take about 1 hour. They will keep for 2–3 days in the fridge.

Gaz's
BOOZY
MINCE PIES

There's something extra-Christmassy and special about making your own mince pies from scratch. So get those Christmas tunes playing and have a fun time making these.

FOR THE FILLING
300g (scant 2 cups) mixed dried fruit
2 eating apples (such as Braeburn), grated
juice and zest of 1 orange
juice and zest of ½ lemon

120ml (½ cup) agave nectar
1 tsp allspice
60ml (¼ cup) vegan-friendly brandy

FOR THE PASTRY
1 quantity of sweet pastry (page 142)
caster (superfine) sugar, for sprinkling

Makes
12

Cooks In
35 minutes

Difficulty
5/10

Thoroughly combine all the filling ingredients in a large mixing bowl. Cover the bowl and leave the mixture overnight, or for at least 12 hours, stirring every now and then, if possible. Spoon the mince pie filling into sterilized jars (page 112) – it will keep for 2 months in the fridge.

When you're ready to make the mince pies, grease a non-stick bun tin and preheat the oven to 180°C (350°F). Sprinkle a little flour onto your work surface and roll out the pastry to around 3mm (⅛in) thick.

Cut 12 circles to fit your bun tray, line the holes and pop a teaspoonful of pie filling mixture into each one. Cut out the tops for each one – in shapes if you wish – and place over the filling, pressing the edges gently to seal. Sprinkle over some caster sugar and bake for 12–15 minutes, or until golden.

Let the mince pies cool before serving with my Mulled wine (page 170) or packaging up to give to friends and family.

Mulled
★ ★ WINE ★ ★

You can easily make this into mulled cider instead. Just use two 500ml (17fl oz) bottles of vegan cider instead of the red wine.

1 75cl bottle vegan red wine
juice and peel of 2 clementines
1 vanilla pod, seeds scraped out
50g (¼ cup) caster (superfine) sugar
4 cloves
2 cinnamon sticks
1 tsp grated nutmeg
1 bay leaf
2 star anise

Serves
4

Cooks In
20 minutes

Difficulty
2/10

GF

Pour half the bottle of wine into a large saucepan. Squeeze the juice of the clementines in and add the peel (it adds great flavour). Add the vanilla pod and seeds. Add the rest of the ingredients.

Place the saucepan over a medium heat and bring it to a simmer. Simmer for 10 minutes to let all the flavours infuse. After 10 minutes, pour in the rest of the wine and turn the heat down low. Once piping hot, serve in your favourite Christmas mugs or in heatproof glasses.

Photograph on **page 169**.

INDEX

ACKNOWLEDGEMENTS

I feel so grateful to be able to release a second book inside a year of my first book, *Vegan 100*. It's been tough, and a huge amount of work has gone into making it happen, but having some amazing people around me has helped make my dream become a reality.

I would first like to thank my amazing family: Mum, Dad and my sister Charlotte. Thank you for the love and support you constantly give me, for letting me use your cars, take over your kitchen, live at home and for the encouragement you give me when times are hard.

Giorgia, you have been the ultimate support since more or less the start. I wouldn't be in this position if it wasn't for you. You got me through the toughest points of my life and helped me during all the shoots and have been the best of friends. THANK YOU x

Dave and Olly, thank you for putting up with my creative demands and making my YouTube videos beautiful.

To my great friend Joe, thanks again for your help during the photoshoots making this book, couldn't have done it without you.

Thanks so much to my agent and friend Zoe, for making this book happen at short notice. You're the greatest help every day, thanks for putting up with my constant nagging.

Quadrille, my publisher, thanks for letting me do book two and also for putting up with more of my creative demands. You guys are an amazing team and have really helped me along the way.

Simon Smith, thank you for being a genius again and shooting the food pictures. I learn so much when I work with you. I always have the time of my life, cooking and styling the food at your studio. Sorry for making you always dig out the hard-to-find props.

Thanks so much to Peter, young, genius photographer, for shooting the lifestyle pictures and front cover.

Thanks to all the wonderful brands that support me, from clothing, ingredients and cooking equipment, I appreciate your faith in me.

Finally, to all my YouTube subscribers and social media followers. I'm so appreciative to be able to do what I love and I wouldn't be doing it without your support. So a huge thank you from the bottom of my heart.

Big love,

Gaz

PUBLISHING DIRECTOR Sarah Lavelle
PROJECT EDITOR Amy Christian
COPY EDITOR Samantha Stanley
DESIGNER Maeve Bargman
DESIGN ASSISTANT Emily Lapworth
FOOD PHOTOGRAPHER Simon Smith
LIFESTYLE PHOTOGRAPHER Peter O'Sullivan
PROP STYLING Luis Peral, with Gaz Oakley
FOOD STYLING Gaz Oakley
FOOD STYLING ASSISTANT Joe Horner
PRODUCTION CONTROLLER Nikolaus Ginelli
PRODUCTION DIRECTOR Vincent Smith

Published in 2018 by Quadrille, an imprint of Hardie Grant Publishing

Quadrille
52–54 Southwark Street
London SE1 1UN
quadrille.com

Cataloguing in Publication Data: a catalogue record for this book is available from the British Library.

Text © Quadrille 2018
Food photography © Simon Smith 2018
Design © Quadrille 2018
Victorian Illustrations © Dover Publications, Inc, except on pages; 30, 146, 155 © Shutterstock

Reprinted in 2018 (twice)
10 9 8 7 6 5 4 3

ISBN 978 1 78713 267 2

Printed in China